DATE DUE

NEW JERSEY'S FINANCIAL PROBLEM

New Jersey's Financial Problem

by

Paul J. Strayer

Rutgers University Press

New Brunswick   New Jersey

Manufactured in the United States of America by
Edwards Brothers, Inc., Ann Arbor, Michigan

Contents

NEW JERSEY'S FINANCIAL PROBLEM

CHAPTER I
New Jersey's Financial Problem

The State of New Jersey faces grave fiscal problems. Inadequate revenues, deficits in the support of state activities, and an outmoded tax system have placed New Jersey in an adverse financial position.

The state aid program for education has been based upon an inadequate formulation of the relative capacity of local governments to raise the necessary funds for schools. The result is that New Jersey is saddled with one of the highest property tax burdens among the fifty states. With so little state support given to higher education in comparison with equally wealthy states, over half of New Jersey's students leave the state for their college degrees. As competition for places in colleges and universities increases, and as other state universities impose further restrictions upon the New Jersey resident, this state will have to provide the greater part of higher education for its residents. The State Colleges and the State University therefore must be both enlarged and improved.

Equally serious problems confront the State Highway Department. Once possessing one of the best highway systems in the United States, New Jersey now ranks well toward the bottom. If traffic volume doubles in 1975, as the State Highway Department predicts, increased attention must be directed to the acquisition of rights of way for new highways. One of New Jersey's great difficulties is the fact that years of neglect have placed the state in the position of having to do the necessary expansion in a period of high costs. Such costs will increase as prices for land and construction rise. One alternative which has been suggested to remove some of the burden from the state's highways is the subsidization of a public transportation system. It is doubtful that this will solve the problem, however, since few persons will wish to use common carriers when the automobile is available.

Pressing problems arise also in the state's institutions and agencies. Because of a shortage of personnel and a limited budget allotment, the institutionalized population of New Jersey fares poorly; for the most part patients have been given only custodial care. One of the greatest deficiencies exists in the field of psychiatric care. With a high ratio of patients to doctors and psychiatrists, treatment and rehabilitation for the committed are slow and inadequate. The growth in relief needs poses another problem. Although this increase is probably temporary, it nevertheless raises a serious problem for the state budget.

Recreational facilities are notable for their absence. New Jersey may well be proud of Island Beach, yet because of insufficient appropriations little has been done to realize the potential of this recreational asset. Other parks have felt the same blight: insufficient personnel to manage them properly, too few developed tracts. With a population density second only to that of Rhode Island, there is a definite need for many additional recreational areas in New Jersey.

The Department of Conservation and Economic Development has been turned into one of the most illogical conglomerations yet created by any state. Included in its functions are veterans' affairs, economic promotion, water, parks, fish and game preserves, planning, and a host of other activities. One great defect is the inability of the department to function successfully in its capacity as planner for the state. Here too the problem is one of inadequate appropriation from a restricted budget, and the result is that no one is able to tell the Governor, the legislature, or the public enough about what the state is going to face in the years ahead.

In the matter of water supply there has been no planning beyond the development of Spruce Run and the reservoir at Round Valley. The bond issue voted in the fall of 1958 did provide some funds to investigate water needs. Yet within a few years Northern New Jersey will require additional supplies of water. Land for the next storage basins should be acquired now before the cost of acquisition becomes prohibitive.

In the field of economic development there exists little evidence that New Jersey will hold its own in competition with the more aggressive states. The inadequacy of the staff is the basic problem, and there is no possibility of this condition being corrected as long as the budget is so limited. The priceless asset of the New Jersey beaches will remain in jeopardy until or unless some effort is made to spend the necessary $30 million to assure their permanence. A considerable part of this money could come from the federal government, but the state must allocate some $10 million first.

The Constitution of 1947 made a thorough revision in the legal system of the state. One of its requirements was that local magistrates must be lawyers. But still too many police courts are presided over by judges with too little to do for efficient operation.

Perhaps the greatest failure in the state has been the dearth of real leadership. There has been no Governor since Woodrow Wilson willing to use the executive power vested in the office. The Constitution of 1947 gave greatly increased authority to the Governor, but the situation was not remedied thereby. The precarious balance of power between the two major political parties has prevented succeeding Governors from taking advantage of their theoretically enhanced situations. With the State Assembly often Democratic and the Senate almost constantly Republican, the Governor is in an exceedingly difficult position. And there is lack of leadership from any other source. The influence of the Press and of the leaders in commerce, industry, and finance has produced a negative attitude on the part of the general public toward most state problems.

Even more unfortunate has been the traditional slogan of "no new taxes," for without money state services cannot be adequately supported. This slogan has not prevented the rise in the real estate tax burden, the increase in the gasoline tax, the imposition of the cigarette tax, the recent imposition of the corporation income tax, the increase in the severity of the franchise tax, and the increase in the tax on horse racing. In other words, instead of undertaking a thorough revision of the state tax system the tendency has been to look only a year ahead and do a patchwork job to raise the revenue required for that particular year. An example of this tendency is found in the imposition of the corporation income tax. Given the chance to remove the tax on inventories, the New Jersey Chamber of Commerce wished also to prevent any tax on corporate net income, and in the end found that neither the abolition of the inventory tax nor any other reform was accomplished. Still another tax has been added on corporate income.

Part of the blame for these conditions must be placed with the New Jersey Commission on Tax Policy. Although it represents the varied interests of the state, the Commission has never been willing to suggest a thorough revision of the state tax system. This has been the result of its philosophy, which states that the Commission never will advocate a tax program until it is politically practical to pass it. Yet the lack of a positive program has left the state without a yardstick by which to evaluate the existing tax system. It also reflects the general conservatism of the state on tax policy. Without leadership that would dramatize the need for reform, it would perhaps have been useless to advocate such reform. Still the effort to give the people of the state a plan of tax reform might well have led to a growing awareness of the deficiencies of the existing system.

One serious result of this failure on the part of the Commission is that since the passage of the new corporation income tax New Jersey is no longer an attractive state for industrial location. The Middletown Township[1] case indicates that all municipalities will begin to assess inventories and equipment at full ratio to real estate. The addition of a tax on net corporate income will adversely affect the entire position of certain types of industry. The location of the new United States Steel plant in Pennsylvania was no accident. The company was fearful of the potential tax burden on plant, equipment, and inventories if it were located in New Jersey.

Perhaps one of the greatest problems facing the state is the decline in quality of the civil service. When the top personnel who were hired during the depression of the thirties leave office, little ability will be found among their replacements. It is simply a question of salaries. At the level of stenographers and unskilled workers the problem is not acute, but at the top levels, where imagination and a sharp mind are required to deal with difficult situations, the replacements are not available. If New Jersey is not to suffer in the quality of its top-ranking civil servants, salaries must be raised to a level competitive with those of comparable jobs in private business and industry.

Still another feature of the state situation requires comment. This is the inadequacy of office space now available in Trenton as well as for state use in other parts of New Jersey. Working conditions are miserable and the offices of many of the agencies are spread into five or six locations. In the end the cost to the state would be less if the agencies erected their own buildings, for current rentals make a continuing drain on state funds. Again the question is money. There have been debates over the location of the buildings and their cost, but no concrete proposal has been made. Working conditions can make a great difference

---

1. Switz vs. Middletown Township, 130A.2d15. There were five separate citations.

in the morale of most workers, and so long as present conditions obtain, little can be done to attract to the state government the required personnel.

Still another characteristic of New Jersey is the generally negative attitude taken by the citizens toward the problems of state government. A sizeable percentage of the people are interested in New York or Philadelphia firms and consequently tend to read the New York or Philadelphia newspapers. Consequently few people are well informed about the affairs of their own state, and those who show concern seem to have a reactionary attitude. Too many wealthy commuters live in Northern New Jersey and are primarily interested in the fact that New Jersey has no income tax. Others find the domination of the state Senate a welcome relief from the prospects of higher costs and more state services. Yet, unless the state spends more money, there will be a continued deterioration in the quality of the state's public and governmental services which will lead to a decline in the state's rate of growth.

The problem of leadership reflects in part the disgust that tended to be felt when Frank Hague ran the state. Even when Hague was not openly in power there were occasions when he could make deals with the Republicans and still accomplish his purpose. One such event was the passage of the sales tax in 1935. Introduced by the minority leader of the Assembly, the sales tax was put through without adequate debate and repealed within a few months as the result of a well-organized campaign. The minority leader, a Democrat, received a judgeship. Still another reason for the repeal of that tax was the promise of the Governor, Harold Hoffman, to consider an income tax, but nothing ever came of it. There is little question that a deal had been made between Hague and Hoffman to push the sales tax through.

Granting the difficulties of the state, there remains the problem of resolving them. At the present time, the Governor could appoint special commissions to review the deficiencies of the state and gain support for meeting them. But it seems the job must be left to local businessmen and local citizens' groups. What I now fear is that the state will find the quality of its services declining greatly before the public wakes up to the fact.

In the state over the past year I found the number of persons actively seeking a solution to the unmet needs of the state limited to the members of the League of Women Voters and a few isolated individuals. What we must have is enough public support so the Governor can take the problems of the state to the people. In a state so evenly divided between the Republicans and the Democrats it is extremely difficult for a Governor to take the strong position the Constitution of 1947 permits him. It will take concerted effort by progressive citizens of both parties, putting aside for a while the opportunity for temporary partisan advantage, to place the state on a progressive basis.

Even among labor leaders there exists a general lack of understanding of the state's problems and an unwillingness to give support to the income tax, which would prove most desirable from labor's point of view. The A. F. of L. and the C. I. O. have not been able to resolve their jurisdictional differences, and the labor movement has suffered accordingly. Major problems common to both groups can be resolved only as there is a united labor movement, but as things now stand in New Jersey, there is little likelihood of this being accomplished.

The problem of taxation thus remains one of the most troublesome of the many which beset the state government.

Having no broad-base tax, New Jersey lacks the money for necessary services, yet taxes are not low in this state. Heavy property taxes and taxes adverse to business impede growth. Of particular importance is the severity of the property tax as it affects retired persons and those with low incomes. Sooner or later these people will revolt and prevent any further increase in that tax, and the state must then find a new source of income. Certainly the existing system must be improved if there is to be adequate development of the potentials of the state. And the difficulties of accomplishing this are much greater now because of the heavier federal taxes and the resistance of the public to any further increases in state-levied taxes.

Of all the states, New Jersey has the lowest state tax burden at $50.92 per capita. Nebraska and New Hampshire are not far above New Jersey but they are much poorer states. New Jersey also has the lowest per capita state expenditure—$83.17. The excess of expenditures over taxes represents nontax financing: tolls, tuition, fees, etc. New Jersey also leaves to local government a higher percentage of the costs of schools and other services than does almost any other state government.

New Jersey is the second most densely populated state in the Union. In traffic density it is near the top and well above that of its neighbors, New York and Pennsylvania. The bulk of the population is concentrated in the northern section, with a relatively low density in the southern section except for the Camden area.

Between the two sections is the almost completely uninhabited
pine barrens area.

Approximately two thirds of New Jersey's population lives in
the northern section with its highly congested cities and their
suburbs. Heavy traffic flows through the state on the way up
and down the coast. Also there is a growing volume of traffic
moving west, necessitating the building of a new freeway through
the northern counties. This highway is costing a million dollars
a mile for the right of way.

In spite of these variations in population each county has a
representative in the state Senate, thus granting greater power
to the relatively underpopulated sections. Further difficulties
have arisen because of the failure of the state Assembly to re-
apportion itself to reflect changes in population distribution. No
action has been taken as a result of the 1950 census, and consequently overrepresentation is given to Hudson County and under-
representation to several other counties. Until the legislature
chooses to act, no sanction can be used to force the reapportion-
ment of the Assembly.

In relation to its wealth New Jersey does a miserable job in
meeting its obligations to its citizens. For example, in the field
of education, the state was fourth from the bottom of all the
states in its support of higher education in 1957. In terms of
state aid to the public schools, New Jersey is thirty-seventh
from the top. According to the analysis made by Thad L. Hun-
gate, New Jersey ranked forty-seventh in the year 1951-52 when
its expenditures for higher education are related to per capita
income.[2] There is little inclination to grant the support necessary for the education of the citizens of the state. In 1957 New
Jersey ranked twelfth from the bottom in its grants in support
of education and, with the exception of Connecticut, all of the
other states in the lower bracket were considerably poorer than
New Jersey.

In spite of our great traffic density, highway expenditures per
capita were fourth from the bottom on a per capita basis in
1957. In the categorical public assistance field we were third
from the bottom on a per capita basis the same year. Regarding expenditures for health and hospitals, we were again distin-
guished by finding our state sixteenth from the bottom. The
problem of mental health is growing in importance, yet in 1957
we were twenty-fourth from the bottom, per capita, and again all

2. *A New Basis of Support for Higher Education* (New York, 1957), p. 45.

the states below New Jersey were considerably poorer ones. Even in the field of general control, which represents expenditure for general government service, we find New Jersey twenty-third from the bottom on a percapita basis.

These statistics support the generalization that New Jersey's future well-being is in jeopardy if we do not spend more money and bring better qualified people into government. The backward and irresponsible manner in which the state has side-stepped these issues must be remedied and New Jersey must raise its standards and assume responsibility for the needs of its people.

There is need for a much higher concentration of public parks than in most of the rest of the country. The state-owned parks are not only too few in number, but those we do have are undermanned and suffer from lack of an adequate budget. Compare the total park land of New Jersey with that of Pennsylvania or New York. Our total is some 266,165 acres. In New York, on the other hand, there were more than two and one half million acres in 1938 and undoubtedly more land has been acquired since then. Pennsylvania had over one and one half million acres of land for recreation in the same year. Even along our highways there are few places other than on the Garden State Parkway where a person can turn off the road for a rest or for a simple meal. Most other states have been able to afford such luxuries, but not New Jersey. Especially in the areas of greatest population density, where the need is also greatest, is there a dearth of public recreation facilities.

School yards do not provide the sort of recreation that the public demands, and in the areas of Hudson County, Newark and Elizabeth there are few other open spaces for adult and juvenile recreation. It has been suggested a number of times that some of the meadow land in the Hackensack Valley be converted to public parks. The fact of the matter is that the state has insufficient funds to do the job. A quotation from the latest report on our recreational needs by the State Planning Board is of interest in this connection:

"They state, 'Few states had so much to start with and perhaps no state has despoiled or thrown away so much recreational opportunity as has New Jersey. Our present situation is far from hopeless, but it is sad. It may well be that New Jersey's failure to provide and protect recreational areas and facilities have been more than usually serious because of the State's peculiar circumstances, including a flooding population already reaching a density of 600 people per square mile (second highest among the 49 states); its position in relation to metropolitan areas of New York and Philadelphia; and its possession of an almost too accessible and widely popular ocean beach.' "[3]

In spite of this report little has been done to increase the play space in the state. Island Beach has been acquired but not developed. Other properties have been acquired but not developed. Little if any serious thought has been given to the real needs of the state and practically no program has been worked out to assure the acquisition of the necessary land. Soon land prices will be so high that there will be little chance of getting the required amount.

In addition, little effort has been made to protect the streams and other water preserves of the state. Most of the streams are polluted, and hunting and fishing preserves have been grossly neglected. As a result most of the hunting is done on private property in violation of "no trespassing" signs. Little restocking has been done in the mountain streams of the state. Although the Delaware River above Trenton represents one of the greatest natural park lands of the nation, the state has failed to develop the recreational potential of the Delaware Valley. Few if any swimming beaches have been developed, and the further pollution of the river has not been prevented. The same point can be raised about the potential recreational possibilities of the upper beaches of the Raritan and Passaic Rivers. Even the smaller streams are neglected and many are used as dumps. One of the state's greatest assets is the Delaware and Raritan Canal, but its recreational potential has not been used. Of course, little can be done until more land is acquired, but even now much of the canal can be of great value to the state.

The above adds up to a statement that if New Jersey is to prosper the functions of government will have to receive more attention. Recreation can make a real difference. Planning for the future will make the greatest difference in the basic characteristics of the state. If our highways are not improved soon, the congestion will be so great as to make it impossible for traffic to move within the state.

3. *Where Shall We Play?* A Report on the Outdoor Recreational Needs of New Jersey (New Jersey State Planning Board, 1938), p. 4.

Institutional care is a growing problem and must receive more attention as the aged population increases. Yet the salaries of institutional attendants are far below what they ought to be if we are to maintain the best care that can be given. There is even a possibility that, given better care, the period of institutionalization would be significantly shortened, and the state could save money rather than having to increase its budget for custodial care of the mentally ill and other cases.

Still the greatest need is for planning of the sort that can be done only by a competent staff under competent direction. The growth of school populations can be predicted with a high degree of accuracy. The needs for roads can be estimated almost as well. Parks and other recreational needs can be estimated with reasonable certainty, as can institutional populations. The growth in the requirements for water and other utilities also can be fairly estimated. Population growth is another factor that can be estimated. Such planning is possible only if there exists a reasonably fair tax system and sufficiently high service levels of the state which will attract people of ability.

As population grows there will arise special problems in the urban concentrations. There is little doubt that highly congested areas cost more to run than do more rural areas. Still another problem is that of the decline of the big city and the need for urban renewal and improvement in the quality of education, recreation, and other services available to the mass of the public in the large cities. Neglect of the problems of the large city can lead to a general deterioration of these areas, as the poorer element moves in and the richer people move to the suburbs.

Finally, if New Jersey is not to become a declining area, the people must come to realize that the costs of government are as essential as any other cost, and that good government is bound to cost money.

CHAPTER II

The New Jersey Economy

New Jersey is the eighth-ranking state of the United States in size of labor force. From 1900 to 1950 New Jersey's labor force increased from 758,000 to 2.1 million, a gain of 177 per cent. The total labor force for the country as a whole increased only 107 per cent over the same period. At the beginning of the century New Jersey ranked thirteenth among all the states in size of labor force; at mid-century her rank had risen to eighth. However, the appearance of substantial growth momentum during this 50-year span is somewhat misleading. Actually, at about the end of the 1920's New Jersey's role as one of the pace setters in growth of labor forces among the states came to an end. Since 1930 her labor force growth has closely paralleled that of the national labor force. The year 1930 appears to have marked New Jersey's coming of age as a mature economy.[1]

Since 1947 the annual average number of persons employed in nonagricultural jobs in New Jersey has increased by almost 300,000, reaching the figure of 1,918,000 in 1956. This was a gain of 18.3 per cent in nine years. It was accompanied by an estimated population gain of 16.7 per cent over the same period. (119)

After fifty years of growth and development, New Jersey's over-all economy at mid-century had come to be crucially dependent upon the status and well-being of her manufacturing industries. Only Connecticut and Michigan, among the larger states, showed a higher concentration of labor force in the manufacturing sector. Agriculture had become a specialized activity in the Garden State and claimed only 2.3 per cent of the total labor force in 1950. (121)

As against the over-all growth of 18.3 per cent in nonfarm

1. *The Economy of New Jersey*, A Report Prepared for the Department of Conservation and Economic Development of the State of New Jersey. By: A Group of Rutgers Scholars under the Direction of Professor Salomon J. Flink of the Department of Economics of Rutgers, The State University (Rutgers University Press, 1958). *Growth and Structure of Employment*, by Thomas J. Reynolds, p. 119. The following quotations are from this source with the page references appearing at the end of each.

jobs from 1947 to 1956, manufacturing employment has increased by only 5.6 per cent. Employment in construction has increased by 55.9 per cent in these nine years; in trade, by 33.6 per cent; in services, by 32.0 per cent; in government, by 30.9 per cent; in finance, insurance, and real estate by 28.9 per cent; and in transportation and utilities, by 8.4 per cent. (121)

Yet it is easy to exaggerate the extent of these shifts. Actually from 1947 to 1956 the proportion of manufacturing employment to total nonfarm employment in the state declined only from 47.8 per cent to 42.6 per cent, while the proportion for trade, the second largest sector in volume of employment, increased only from 16.2 per cent to 18.3 per cent. (121)

For the United States as a whole manufacturing jobs have increased by 10.6 per cent since 1947. New Jersey's growth of only 5.6 per cent contrasts badly with California's gain of 66.6 per cent, Florida's gain of 61.4 per cent, Texas' gain of 45.8 per cent, and Georgia's gain of 22.5 per cent. In fact, ten of the seventeen large states outdid New Jersey in the field of manufacturing employment during these nine postwar years. (122)

Nevertheless, on the basis of a general examination, it may be concluded that New Jersey's economy as a whole has indeed fared well up to the present. The first half of the twentieth century has seen this state pass through a long period of dynamic, above-average growth and then evolve into a phase of less spectacular, average performance appropriately described as a "mature economy" stage in her development. The dynamics of the next half century may produce revolutionary changes in the industrial character of the American economy and violent shifts in the regional distribution of economic activity. (123)

The growth trends in New Jersey varied considerably from one industry to another. Employment declined in certain types of production, such as textile, which dominated the industry of New Jersey in the twentieth century and remained so until 1929. Electrical equipment and chemicals increased most rapidly during the forty-eight year period and are now among the first three types of manufacturing. Clothing, not high in value added, came second in rank of employment in 1947 and in first rank of employment according to the 1950 census of population. Employment is now less concentrated in any one class of manufactures than it was in 1899, when 27 per cent of all production workers were in textiles. At present the combined employment

TABLE I

DISTRIBUTION OF LABOR FORCE BY BROAD INDUSTRY DIVISIONS
1900 AND 1950: NEW JERSEY AND THE UNITED STATES,
WITH PERCENTAGE CHANGES BY DIVISIONS,
1900 to 1950

	New Jersey			United States		
	1900	1950	% Change	1900	1950	% Change
Agricultural, forestry and fisheries	10.8	2.3	-0.021	39.1	11.6	-0.0296
Mining	0.5	0.2	-0.40	2.6	1.6	-0.615
Construction	10.4	6.3	-0.605	6.1	6.2	+0.103
Manufacturing	27.8	36.7	+132.01	14.6	25.3	+173.28
Transportation, etc.	9.2	8.0	-0.869	6.6	7.5	+113.63
Trade, finance, etc.	18.7	22.1	+118.18	12.8	21.5	+16.79
Services and public administration	19.5	21.9	+112.30	16.6	23.6	+142.16
Private household	7.7	2.0	-0.0259	6.8	2.5	-0.0367
All other	11.8	19.8	+167.7	10.1	21.2	+209.9
Not reported	3.1	2.5	-.0806	1.3	2.6	+200.0
All industries	100.0	100.0	177.0	100.0	100.0	106.3

in any two of the leading industries is less than 24 per cent of total employment.[2]

Not only is New Jersey a manufacturing state but by far the greatest part of its population lives in urban areas. Of the total population of the state almost seven-eighths, or 86.6 per cent, live in urban areas. This is the next to the highest percentage among all the states and is much higher than the national average of 64 per cent.(1)

By far the greatest percentage of the population lives in the northeastern counties. These counties include 3,165,912 in the

2. John E. Brush, *The Population of New Jersey* (New Brunswick, 1956), p. 44. The following quotations are from this source with the page references appearing at the end of each.

14   NEW JERSEY'S FINANCIAL PROBLEM

TABLE II

TOTAL EMPLOYMENT, NEW JERSEY AND THE UNITED STATES
BY MAJOR ECONOMIC SECTORS, 1956

	Total Employment		Per Cent Distribution	
	N. J.	U. S.	N. J.	U. S.
Agriculture	51.7	8,122	2.6	13.5
Mining	4.4	816	0.2	1.4
Construction	105.4	2,993	5.4	5.0
Manufacturing	817.8	16,905	41.5	28.2
Durable goods	453.3	9,825	23.0	16.4
Nondurable goods	364.5	7,080	18.5	11.8
Trade	351.0	11,292	17.8	18.8
Wholesale	88.3	3,032	4.5	5.1
Retail	262.8	8,260	13.3	13.7
Finance, insurance, etc.	81.2	2,303	4.1	3.8
Government	202.8	7,178	10.3	12.0
Federal	50.4	2,209	2.6	3.7
State and local	152.5	4,969	7.7	8.3
	1,970.0	60,000	100.0	100.0

northeastern region and 327,591 in the Camden region, or 65.5 and 6.8 per cent respectively, of the state's population. Three smaller urbanized areas are at Trenton, with 179,240 persons, Atlantic City with 105,083, and at Penns Grove on the Delaware River (opposite Wilmington, Del.), a small urban territory with 15,061 persons. Together these three urbanized areas account for another 6.2 per cent of the state population and bring the total in the five urbanized areas to 3,792,887, or 78.4 per cent of the population. The balance of 393,320, or 8.1 per cent, is found in other urban places outside of the five areas mentioned. (2&3)

It is also true that the northeastern counties have by far the highest concentration of wealth in the state. The five urbanized counties of the Northeast all had income well above the state average of $3,289 in 1950. Bergen and Union were at the top of the income ladder with 80 per cent of all families receiving incomes above $2,000 in 1949 and the median income being about

TABLE III

NONAGRICULTURAL EMPLOYMENT IN NEW JERSEY BY MAJOR INDUSTRY DIVISIONS, 1939, 1947 and 1956 WITH PERCENTAGE DISTRIBUTION AND PERCENTAGE CHANGES

Division	New Jersey Number (000)			Per Cent Distribution			Per Cent Gain		
	1939	1947	1956	1939	1947	1956	1939 to 1947	1939 to 1956	1947 to 1956
Mining	3.8	4.0	4.4	0.3	0.2	0.2	+5.3	+15.8	+10.0
Construction	43.6	67.6	105.4	3.5	4.2	5.5	+55.0	+141.7	+55.9
Manufacturing	578.6	774.4	817.8	46.5	47.8	42.8	+33.8	+41.3	+5.6
Transportation & utilities	109.1	142.1	154.0	8.8	8.8	8.0	+30.2	+41.2	+8.4
Trade	213.9	262.7	351.0	17.2	16.2	18.3	+22.8	+64.1	+33.6
Finance & insurance	57.6	63.0	81.2	4.6	3.9	4.2	+9.4	+41.0	+28.9
Services	115.4	152.8	201.7	9.3	9.4	10.5	+32.4	+74.8	+32.0
Government	122.3	154.9	202.8	9.8	9.6	10.6	+26.7	+65.8	+30.9
	1,244.3	1,621.6	1,918.4	100.0	100.0	100.0	30.3	54.2	18.3

$4,000. In these same northeastern counties more than 25 per cent of the families received over $5,000 annually. (57 & 85)

Among the many other industry groups reported in the census of population, only the finance, insurance, and real estate group exhibits a disproportionately high concentration of employment in New Jersey, 5.0 per cent as compared to 3.4 per cent in the United States as a whole. Data available on employment within the state indicate that only about half the persons in this group were actually employed in New Jersey. Newark's financial and insurance business cannot account for the unusual concentration of this group in New Jersey. It must result from the large number of residents of New Jersey who travel to New York daily to engage in the banking and brokerage business. Finance, insurance, and real estate businesses support less than one seventh of the people in manufacturing. But it is significant that this industrial group shows nearly half again as much concentration as in the nation as a whole. Consequently, there is relatively as much concentration of employment in this group as in manufacturing. (48)

As indicated in the figures cited, the state lags in the field of wholesale and retail trade. There is reason to believe that this is due to the large concentration of retail establishments in New York and Philadelphia. But it is in agriculture, forestry, fisheries, and mining that New Jersey falls short most. The basic problem now is to find new industries to replace those which fail or are bought out by larger concerns. The climate is no longer favorable to such industries, as a new corporation income tax has been added to the inventory tax and the tax on machinery and equipment. Because property tax rates are high, many individuals feel that they can no longer afford to live in New Jersey. Few firms find a high rate of property taxation to their liking and few appreciate the lack of state services that are to be found in many other states of comparable wealth. If I were to estimate I would venture to say that New Jersey no longer has a competitive advantage.

The immediate need is for a complete revision of the state tax system so that adequate service levels can be justified and the local schools, colleges, and university can look upon the rest of the country as equals. If New Jersey does not find some means of support for essential services, its problems will continue to increase and residence in the state will prove to be a liability rather than an asset. Most state services are meager in relation to the ability to pay for them. The recreation program is almost completely lacking. Water and highways are suffering from inadequate support. Institutions and agencies are doing a poor job. More vocational education is required. More advanced work at the State University is essential if New Jersey is to prosper. More attention must be paid to the civil service or its quality will deteriorate to the level of the worst in the country. What we are willing to pay for we can support. There is no excuse for the low salaries paid in Trenton or for those paid to the men and women who care for the unfortunates in state hospitals. There is no excuse for the poor support of education.

What New Jersey needs is an immediate and thorough review of its tax system and a plan for basic reform. Each year the legislature attempts to get by another year without any reform of what is one of the worst tax systems of any wealthy state. The lack of leadership leaves the state without the dramatic appeal that could make the difference. Granting the power of the leaders in the field of commerce, trade, and industry and of the press, the lack of any desire to reform the state system is pitiful and unjustified.

Even in the area of personal income growth the state has tended to expand less rapidly than the rest of the United States. The relative decline of New Jersey income is due, in part, to the very high rates of income growth in the less-industrialized, low-income regions of the southern and southwestern United States. Also responsible for the relative decline of per capita income are forces peculiar to the New Jersey economy, and it is in this area that conscious policies designed to promote a more vigorous growth of the state's income might meet with success.

In 1954 the eight leading industrial counties contained 85 per cent of all manufacturing establishments and also attracted 85 per cent of the new entrants to the state's manufacturing complex. Beyond the "Big Eight" a significant feature was the ability of some of the state's so-called "nonindustrial" counties to attract some of the larger new manufacturing establishments; of the 112 new entrants set up to employ 50 or more persons, 26 settled in these counties: Atlantic, Burlington, Cumberland, Gloucester, Hunterdon, Monmouth, Salem, Somerset, and Warren. In order of attraction, the three most important among these nonindustrial counties were Monmouth, Burlington, and Atlantic; they attracted 45 per cent of the new entrants that did not settle in the eight most industrialized counties. This

suggests that a trend has set in with the development of the Delaware Valley and that the new industrial development of these
counties will be the area of most rapid growth in the future of
New Jersey industry. With low flow control and the preparation
of dams and other means of flood control, the Delaware Valley
should prove to be one of the most interesting areas for future
development.[3]

A zipper manufacturer who moved from Connecticut to a rural area of the state thought New Jersey's growth would be retarded by "the lack of an adequate number of trade schools in
rural areas."

Another problem has been the growth of a sizable group that
expected labor conditions to be better than were actually realized. Should the disappointments of this group be communicated
to prospective citizens, the state's growth might be retarded.
(257)

As already mentioned, the state should study the possibility
of achieving a labor force advantage through programs that will
increase the skills and productivity of workers. Complaints
about these labor characteristics appeared frequently. (257)

In the field of labor relations "the rate of growth of the labor
movement in New Jersey between 1939 and 1956 exceeded that
experienced in the country as a whole. It is estimated that organized labor in this State has more than tripled its membership since 1939 . . . the relative growth of union membership in
New Jersey exceeded every state but Michigan."[4]

In the field of agriculture "New Jersey has the most intensive agricultural production of any state in the nation. The
State's cash receipts from farm marketings per acre exceeded
all other states. The Garden State's cash income from farm
marketings has more than tripled during the past two decades
and in 1956 totaled $333.6 million. While part of this increase
was due to rising farm prices, it is estimated that the physical
volume of farm production in New Jersey is now 75 per cent
higher than in the pre-World War II period from 1935 to 1939.
This is something of a record for a state whose farm population

---

3. *Manufacturing Industries*, by Horace J. DePodwin and Morton M.
Binenstock. Flink, *op. cit.*, pp. 247-248. The following quotations are from
this source with the page references appearing at the end of each.
    4. *Labor Relations*, by Allan Weisenfeld. Flink, *op. cit.*, p. 295.

represents only a little over 2 per cent of the total population."[5]

Farm wage rates in New Jersey increased 266 per cent from
1940 to 1956, while the prices received by farmers for farm
products rose only 93 per cent in the same period. The shortage of farm labor has been intensified by the steady migration
of farm labor to higher paying industrial jobs in the state.

Another problem facing the New Jersey farmer is the "cost-
price squeeze." Prices received by New Jersey farmers have
declined 15 per cent since 1952, while there has been little or
no drop in the cost of production. (510)

In 1956, 37 per cent of the state's farm cash income was accounted for by poultry, including eggs, chickens, broilers, and
other poultry. Receipts from eggs alone represented 31 per
cent of total farm income while broilers accounted for 3 per
cent, chickens 2 per cent, turkeys and other poultry 1 per cent.

Truck crops, including sweet potatoes, accounted for 19 per
cent of total farm receipts, the same percentage as dairy products. A portion of the 6 per cent receipts from meat animals
is really associated with the dairy branch of agriculture, so that
the dairy business ranks second and vegetables rank third in
terms of cash receipts. All fruits represented 5 per cent, while
potatoes were 2 per cent and field crops 3 per cent of the 1956
total cash income. Items accounted for in the remaining 9 per
cent consisted almost entirely of greenhouse and nursery products. (515)

The state's dairy cattle have the second highest rate of milk
production per cow in the nation. New Jersey's average annual
yield of 7,850 pounds of milk per cow was exceeded only by
California, where production averaged 8,600 pounds per cow.
The New Jersey rate of production per cow is 30 per cent above
the United States average. (521)

It is clear that unless the state increases its offerings of
services, improves its highways, gains more water, develops
more parks and other facilities for the people, New Jersey will
become a declining region. The reason for this failure has been
the tradition of no new taxes. Little can be done until the level
of State services has been radically improved. Little will be

5. *The Agricultural Economy,* by Allen G. Waller and John W. Carncross.
Flink, *op. cit.,* p. 509. The following quotations are from this source with
the page references appearing at the end of each.

accomplished until there is a thorough revision of the state revenue system so that instead of one of the worst systems of taxation we can be proud of one of the better tax systems of the nation.

On a competitive basis there is little to be said for the way in which we now raise our revenues. Newark is one of the highest tax areas of the nation and will become increasingly so unless levies are more broadly based. The allocation formula used in the computation of the corporate income tax also works to the disadvantage of the state. We are now one of the highest taxed states of the nation in spite of the low level of state collections. To correct this disadvantage a commission should be appointed to make a thorough study of the entire revenue system of the state. Tax lightning can and will hit many small business firms, to their great disadvantage. The inventory tax should be repealed. The newer forms of taxation, such as sales tax and income tax, should be considered. Only in this way can the state keep pace with inflation, as it is only these taxes that reflect inflationary developments.

CHAPTER III

Financing Education in New Jersey

The per capita payments per school child in New Jersey are second only to New York; yet the problem faced by this state in financing education for its children is caused by the enormous difference in sums which the northern part of the state spends for public education in contrast to the southern part. For example, while Hudson County spends an average per student of $428.26 and Essex spends $415.38, Cumberland County spends only $216.93, Camden County $267.90 and Gloucester County $269.93. There are individual districts within these counties that spend even less, as found in Runnemede in Camden County which spent only $196.75 per student enrolled in its schools. Many other communities spend less than the county average, which is based on the total spent by all communities divided by the weighted average of all school districts in the county.

In contrast to Mississippi which has 624 children 5 to 17 years of age per 1,000 adults of 21-64, New Jersey has only 352. Only New York has fewer, with 339. Considering this low ratio of school-age children to productive workers in the age group between 21 and 64, and considering the wealth of the state, the amount of state support for education should be greater.

In spite of the wealth of the state, there are many deficiencies in its educational program. The most conspicuous deficiency is the lack of adequate support for the state university and other colleges. Even at the elementary and secondary levels there is an inadequate amount of state support for local school districts. Some districts have an assessed valuation per pupil of as little as $2,390, while others have as much as $200,000. With a minimum grant of $50 per pupil and a total expenditure of only $24,330,659 (for the year 1959) the need for a more generous system of state support is evident. In terms of the national picture New Jersey ranks thirty-seventh in the amount of state aid given to local districts. Of the industrial states only Massachusetts ranks below New Jersey.

The traditional neglect of local functions by the state will continue until new revenue sources are found. The growing opposition to high property tax rates and the failure of some seventy-one school budgets at the most recent election suggest a need for more state aid. Unless this is forthcoming even more budgets will fail another year and there will be even more neglect of the basic responsibility of the state to provide the best education possible for its children. The wealthy communities can afford the best education because of the low tax rates that tend to prevail in such districts, but the poorer districts have seen a growing resistance to the imposition of higher and higher tax rates on property. It is important to realize that New Jersey collects the smallest amount of all the forty-eight states from its state tax system and depends almost entirely upon the property tax and indirect levies imposed upon articles consumed by the average person.

Special problems arise in those areas that have been showing rapid growth. It is in these areas that the sudden need for new school buildings will cause the tax rate to rise in spectacular fashion. Further complications arise due to the increase in the number of retired persons and their objection to any upward movement in the property tax rate. In a period of inflation most retired individuals find their pensions inadequate and are bound to resist further increases in property tax rates.

Resistance to the property tax has been growing over the years. It reflects the poor assessment practices that are common over most of the United States. It also reflects the more widespread knowledge that the property tax is outmoded in a period when more and more of the wealth of the country is in wages and salaries paid to individuals or is in the form of investment income. Another reason for the decline in the value of the property tax is the growing awareness of the superior revenue-raising powers of state government and the need for more equitable distribution of the costs of government. Some communities within the state find it simply impossible to finance an adequate educational program.

The need for state aid is reinforced by the tendency for industrial and bedroom communities to become separated. When this occurs there is little chance for the bedroom community to gain the advantage of the industrial taxes unless the state imposes a broadly based tax and redistributes the revenue to local governments. Finally, in face of the difficulties of raising sufficient sums at either state or local level, we must ask whether the next move will not be to request aid from the federal government in equalizing educational opportunity over the whole United States. At the moment there seems to be great resistance to federal aid, due in part to the segregation issue. But if the quality of educational opportunity continues to deteriorate, as now seems likely, federal assistance for education may become an issue of real importance.

Another measure of the effort expended by state government for education is found in the fact that New Jersey spent only 2.44 per cent of personal income payments for education in 1956-57. This compares to 4.09 per cent in South Dakota and 4.06 per cent in New Mexico and Wyoming, and places New Jersey thirty-fourth in the ranking of all the states in its expenditure for education of elementary and secondary school pupils.

The growing resistance to property taxation and the low ranking of the state grants-in-aid suggest that there will be an increasing demand for state assistance in the financing of local school districts. Add to this the need for much greater support of the State University and of the State Colleges, and it is clear that current needs cannot be met by use of the inadequate tax system that now exists. If, in addition, a community college program is undertaken to give terminal education to approximately half the students of the state, the need for new tax sources becomes even more obvious.

Like most states New Jersey has been showing an increase in the school population due to the rise in the birth rate during the postwar period. And migration will bring others to the state in large numbers. In the next five years the size of the school enrollment will depend upon the rate of migration. But we are certain that there will be at least 200,000 more children by 1963. This estimate is based upon the existing population and a small factor for migration into the state. Let us assume that costs remain at current levels, which is a poor assumption due to the rise in teachers' salaries, in building costs, and also in the cost of materials and books: the 200,000 larger enrollment will increase costs to approximately $150 million.

The cost of construction also will continue to rise if only to make up for certain deficiencies in the existing plant and equipment and to take care of the growth in enrollment that is certain to take place. Again using current costs, the expansion to take care of new enrollments will cost the local governments $147 million to house the expanded elementary enrollment and $147 million to house the expected increase in the high schools of the state. Owing to the differentials in the cost of elementary and high school buildings, a figure of $1,200 was used for each pupil in the elementary schools and $2,150 for the high schools. These add to a total expenditure of some $294 million over the next five years. I assume current prices. If prices rise, more will have to be spent. The 1958-59 school year has been one in which there has been a decline in school construction due to the recession and the rise in the property tax. In view of the fact that school costs will continue to rise so long as inflation is the rule, these costs will probably be exceeded in the next five years. In addition, the cost of the land needed for the schools is going to rise along with the increasing density of population.

One of our needs is the abandonment of the small high school in favor of large regional high schools. If this is done, further increases in the cost of construction will be placed upon the state and local communities. The need to eliminate the small high school is pressing in certain areas where the population is less concentrated than in the northern part of the State. A decent educational program cannot be run in a high school with fewer than 800 to 1,000 students. Yet many schools in Southern New Jersey have as few as 100 to 300 students. It is in these schools that science becomes too expensive to finance, a differentiated program results in too small classes, and the average level of instruction becomes diluted because of the difficulty of separating students according to ability.

If the Delaware Valley experiences the sort of expansion that is possible, most of these estimates will fall far short of what must actually be spent. Studies are now being made of the potential of the Delaware Valley and the possible industrial development of the area. Given good water supplies and low-flow control as a result of dams in the upper reaches of the Delaware, the potential of the area is tremendous. This is the one part of New Jersey that has room for real industrial expansion and the proper port facilities to support the growth of industry.

Another way of estimating the cost of schools in New Jersey is to compare the costs with those in New York. As already indicated, the greater part of the population of the state is located in the northeastern counties. These areas are directly competitive with Westchester County and Long Island, where teachers' salaries have been raised substantially above those paid in New Jersey. In many of these areas teachers are currently receiving as much as $9,000 to $10,000 a year. If we are to keep our best teachers, salaries must be made comparable. In New York the amount of state aid is fixed at a minimum of $125 per child and the high schools receive a grant one and a quarter times as much due to the greater expense of high school education. This type of program will be required in New Jersey if all students are to receive what should be spent for the education of all the children of the state.

At the present time the state maintains a $200 foundation program below which no community may fall. It also pays a minimum of $50 for each child enrolled in school.[1] The New Jersey Education Association estimates that the cost of a $300 foundation program with a minimum of $75 for each child would cost the state about $77 million. As enrollments increase the costs would rise. No one has yet estimated the cost of a $400 foundation program, which would be much more in line with what the state should now be spending. We may be assured that it would be more than a third more than the $300 foundation program due to the larger grants that would be necessary in the many areas with a tax base that cannot finance an adequate educational program. State grants are made in relation to the size of the tax base available to the local community, after equalization. There is little question but that many more communities would become eligible for larger grants because their tax base fails to increase proportionately with the increase in the size of the foundation program. We are now taxing property owners at a record high of $773,123,000 a year.

If the industrial expansion of New Jersey continues and the Delaware Valley grows as expected, the tax base will increase, The question then arises as to whether it will increase in relation to the rising costs of education. We must also remember that other costs of government also are going to rise as more individuals require institutional aid, as the population grows

1. The foundation program for each school district in each school year shall be $200 per pupil in average daily enrollment. For this purpose: The local fair share of the foundation school program shall be determined for each school district as a sum equal to 5 mills per dollar upon the equalized valuation of the taxing district or districts within the school district, as certified by the director of the State Division of Taxation for the year in which the calculation is made plus 25 per cent of the amount of shared taxes payable to each municipality within the district as certified by such director.

Equalization aid shall be paid to each district in the amount of the excess of the foundation program over the local fair share, provided that each district shall be paid not less than $50 per pupil.

older, and as more attention is given to such problems as urben renewal. Between 1951 and 1956 the property tax base increased by $6 billion. Other taxes also have risen, as more severe rates have been applied to the same base. The real question is whether this will be sufficient to balance the state budget. If inflation ever stops, the problem of the increase in the size of the property tax base will depend upon the industrial and population growth of the state. There is at least some reason to believe that the recent increases will not be repeated short of war or other circumstances with as great an impact as war. In the face of these facts the property tax base will not increase as rapidly as it has in the past, and the state will have to provide for much greater aid in one form or another.

It seems clear that to finance the increased cost of education over the next few years some greater assistance from the state will be required. If the state does not give this assistance, a decline in the quality of the educational experience will occur at the cost of future growth and the development of a well-qualified work force.

The other taxes imposed by the state also have risen in recent years. The tax on gasoline has increased from $43 million in 1952 to $56 million in 1957. Unfortunately there is a discouraging element to this growth, for from 1956 to 1957 the tax yield increased only $352,000, a rate well below that achieved in earlier years. Another important tax is that imposed upon the corporation as a franchise tax. Although the State Tax Policy Commission recommended a revision of the law to remove the tax on inventories, the legislature decided to add a corporation income tax without correction for any of the inequities of the past. The difficulty of the tax on corporation machinery and equipment and on inventories is that the practices of the various communities vary from full assessment to no assessment. In other words, it is a tax that tends to be negotiated by the assessor and the business firm. In addition, certain types of firms find that a tax on inventories makes New Jersey an unattractive state in which to locate. A prime example of this is the decision of United States Steel to locate its new plant in Pennsylvania rather than in New Jersey. If, as a result of the Middletown Township case, full value of machinery and equipment and of inventories is assessed, New Jersey will become a most unattractive state for industry.

Another important tax is the tax on pari-mutuel betting. In 1957 this tax yielded $23.6 million. Although this tax was increased in 1954, the yield has not risen in proportion to the increase. In 1952 the yield was $22.9 million and in the year of increased rates the yield declined to the level of previous years. If the recession continues, there is danger that the pari-mutuel tax will decline even further in fiscal year 1960.

Another important source of state revenue has been the tax on cigarettes. This tax also was increased in the fiscal year 1955-56 from 3 cents a pack to 5 cents a pack. Adjusting for the change in rates, there has been almost no change in the yield of this tax since it was first imposed. In other words, there is little likelihood that there will be any substantial increase in the yield of the cigarette tax in the years to come, except as the population expands.

The other major sources of state revenue include the following: motor vehicle fees, which yielded $73 million in 1958; the alcoholic beverage tax, which produced $19.7 million in 1958; the transfer inheritance tax, which produced $16.5 million in 1958; the tax on foreign insurance companies, which yielded $14 million in 1958; the tax on the main stem and franchise of the railroads, which produced $4.3 million in 1958; the tax on domestic insurance companies, which yielded $700,000 in 1958. In each case the year cited is the fiscal year ending June 30, 1958, and in all cases the figures are estimated for that period. Other sources include beverage licenses, bus excise taxes, tenement house supervision, hotel fire safety inspection fees, division of weights and measures, professional examining boards, and beauty culture control licenses. Together these sources produce $1.7 million.

In most cases the estimates for the fiscal year 1959 are below those for 1958 due to the recession. We must also remember that the growth of state revenues over the past five years has been $59 million less than the increased cost of education will be at a minimum over the next five years. Considering the need for more expenditures for other purposes, the difficulties of the state are made obvious. The growth has also been affected by the rate increases previously mentioned and would have been less if rates had not been increased.

The problems of financing education will be made more difficult as a result of the need for new buildings and a substantial addition to the debt service of most local districts. Between 1951 and 1957 the total debt of school districts increased by almost $400 million. If the needs of the future are to be met, at least $120 million must be spent each year to take care of expanded enrollments and to replace substandard classrooms or to avoid double sessions. If costs rise, as may be anticipated, the outlays may be even larger. The importance of debt service can be illustrated by reference to the growth of debt service charges from $14,716 million in 1951 to $30,942 million in 1957. Let us assume that school districts will increase their debt by $120 million a year for the next five years. The increase in the interest cost and amortization will amount to approximately $10,909 million, assuming that the average bond is for twenty years and that the interest cost is 3 per cent. Some communities will have paid off debts incurred in earlier years, and thus the cost may not rise to this full amount. But if either costs increase or school population increases more rapidly than expected, the costs could be substantially greater.

If we assume that the cost of education is going to increase as salaries are raised and a greater effort is made to serve the need for advanced work for the able student, the possibility of financing these costs without a substantial increase in the property tax rate or a very generous increase in the amount of state aid becomes remote. The protests of the local property taxpayer are now well established and have tended to keep the cost of education from rising as much as it should. It is clear that the additional sums must come from more state aid. We also know that the state's current revenue system is inadequate to finance any such increase. A thorough revision of the tax structure is required if the state is not to neglect its educational responsibilities.

College Requirements

A recent report of the New Jersey State Board of Education has reviewed the college needs of the state until 1965. The pattern is the same as that found in the schools, except that the deficiency is much greater. The report suggests the expenditure of $82,550,000 for new construction but believes that only $65,550,000 will be a burden on the taxpayer because the carrying charges of the dormitories can be borne by student fees. The program of the New Jersey State Board of Education is a modest one. It proposes places for only 12,552 additional students by 1963, or approximately the doubling of existing enrollments. Several factors suggest that the need will be substantially greater in the period covered. First, there is the fact that most of the state universities in other states are facing a similar expansion of their own enrollments and are not going to be anxious to subsidize the residents of New Jersey. Second, many state institutions have raised fees for out-of-state students, so that there will be pressure to go to a home state institution rather than one outside the state. Third, the report suggests that the expansion plans of the private institutions in New Jersey will prove successful. Two facts argue against this possibility. The first is that the cost of government is not likely to decline and the possibility of gaining the sort of endowment required to run a first-class institution is made difficult so long as this situation continues. The other difficulty is that if expansion is based on a shoestring the quality of the resulting education will be well below what the state should support. Finally there is danger that the percentage of students wishing to go to college may be much greater than the 35 per cent figure used in the report.

Another expense that must be recognized is operating costs. At the present time these amount to slightly over $18 million annually. If enrollments are to double, or possibly rise even more, these costs will more than double. The need for more expenditure will develop, because college teachers' salaries will rise in the period of shortage that is immediately before us. The real question remains: are the qualified students of the state going to get the sort of education the state should offer or is the sixth wealthiest state of the nation going to give an inadequate educational opportunity to its youth? The decision is one that will be determined by the action taken in the next year.

Another study of the growth of college needs was completed by Marshall P. Smith, of the faculty of the Trenton State Teachers College.[2] His evidence is much more discouraging, as he estimates that by 1963 enrollment will triple--from 22,000 to 66,000. He also estimates that few of those wanting to go to college can find places in out-of-state institutions, suggesting that the increase will be held to 2,000 students in the period until 1963. Even more discouraging is the prospect for 1963, when one out of every three young poeple wanting to go to college will find no place; in 1973 one out of every two young people wanting to go to college will find no place. He suggests that, according to present plans for expansion of both public and private col-

2. A Publication of the New Jersey State Board of Education, Marshall P. Smith, Survey Director, *The Closing Door to College,* 1960-1970 (Trenton, 1956).

leges, there will be 83,000 New Jersey students with no place to
go in 1973.

In this same study the emphasis is upon the development of a
strengthened State University of some 25,000 students. Emphasis would be on research, professional training, and teaching
facilities. It is pointed out that about half of New Jersey's students want to do some graduate work and the out-of-state institutions cannot carry the full load. A second part of the program
would be the development of engineering colleges for about
10,000 students. The state needs stronger and more extensive
facilities on both graduate and undergraduate levels. A third
part of the program involves the expansion of four-year colleges to take care of 35,000 students. A final part of the program includes the development of community colleges for some
30,000 students. These would give opportunity to many students
who otherwise would be deprived of college-level work because
of the expense.

In addition, more thought needs to be given to scholarship
programs and better guidance programs in the schools, as well
as to better use of existing facilities. All this will cost money,
and the cost to the citizens of New Jersey will rise from the
level of $34.4 million paid either personally or through taxes to
$84.6 million by 1963 and to $155 million by 1973. But even in
1973 the total cost of the higher education program will be only
3/4 cent of the citizen's dollar income in that year, for the purpose of instruction and administrative cost. In 1973 the cost of
buildings will amount to 1/17 cent of the total personal income
of the state for that year. Certainly these costs are not too high
to assure our children the educational opportunity that we want
them to have. As a matter of fact, only as we spend for education will we see our state keep pace with those states that are
achieving the most rapid rate of economic development. Also
the growing complexity of modern society requires more highly
educated individuals capable of solving the more complex issues
that have to be faced in the modern world.

The real question facing the state is the quality of the educational experience it offers to its youth. These individuals will
be the future leaders of the community. The growth of technological advance in New Jersey requires that the state give the
extensive college program required and also advanced work
well beyond the college level. If we do not provide such opportunities for the children of the state, New Jersey will pay the
price for years to come.

If we do what we should, we will reduce the number of class-es taught by the average teacher, increase the amount of time he can devote to strengthening the knowledge of his field of ma-jor interest, and pay teachers enough so that they do not have to work after school or in the summers. This suggests that it will become necessary to increase substantially the amount of state aid if we are to do what the best educational doctrine suggests. Of course some communities will want to do more than a mini-mum program, and they should be encouraged to do so. Other communities will do no more than the state requires. This sug-gests that, if an adequate educational program is to be offered to the children and college students of New Jersey, expenditure will have to be increased from the $200 foundation program to one of at least $400 dollars and that the State Colleges and the State University will see their budgets greatly increased. Cur-rent levels of support permit an adequate program in the wealthy communities but discourage the poorer ones from even attempting to raise their level of preparation. There is no reason why the children in the poorer communities should lack the full advantages offered to those in the wealthier areas. There is no question of the ability of the state to finance such a program without imposing taxes at higher rates than are current in many neighboring states.

Community Colleges

Another recommendation of the New Jersey State Board of Education was the development of community colleges for those who wish to get a terminal education and for those who will transfer to the upper division of a four-year college. In each case the decision regarding the need for such a college would be left to the local community; but state grants-in-aid would be made available to such institutions, if the decision of the com-munity was favorable. It is estimated that the cost of the oper-ating budget would be approximately $600 per student. There would also be the cost of buildings and of land acquisition. Suc-cessful community college programs of this kind have been de-veloped in many states of the Union and have proved to be ex-cellent preparation both for colleges and for jobs. The speed with which such a program develops will be determined in large measure by the type of assistance the state offers to the com-munities that wish to undertake the program. It is doubtful that much will happen within the next five years unless there is a

radical revision of the state tax system. Since there is no sign
that such a revision is going to take place, I doubt that much will
happen for some years to come.

Building Aid

One of the most serious difficulties facing many of the local
districts is the cost of borrowed money. Many poorer communities have had to pay as much as 4 and 5 per cent to raise the
money required for their school buildings. If the state were to
grant sums to local communities at rates not more than 1 per
cent above the rate at which the state can borrow, many of these
communities could greatly reduce their debt payments. I would
much prefer to see such action rather than the creation of
school authority with power to borrow in the open market at the
best rates they could obtain. The benefit of state borrowing is
that it has the effect of greatly reducing the rate of interest as
the result of the tax exemption given to state and local bonds. I
also dislike the use of authorities because of the removal of this
device from the regular control of the state or local government. Although some authorities are well run, there is always
the chance that they will be manned by political favorites and
become corrupt.

Conclusion

We may conclude this section by suggesting that the financing
of education in the State of New Jersey has been too little and
too late. The elementary school, the high school, and the colleges have been neglected due to inadequate revenues. The
amount of state grants-in-aid must be increased. The longer
the state delays its effort to bring its schools and colleges up to
standard the more costly the job will become. In the meantime
failure to make provision for educational opportunities of our
youth has placed New Jersey in an unenviable position of short-
changing the future leaders of the state. If we are to prosper,
there is no more important job than the education of the children
of the state to their fullest capacity.

CHAPTER IV

Division of Conservation and Economic Development

The Division of Conservation and Economic Development has been made a dumping ground for many of the agencies and bureaus for which there is no other place. A list of the varied functions included within the agency supports this contention. It includes such varied functions as the Division of Planning and Development, the Morris Canal and Banking Company, New Jersey Pilot Commissioners, Division of Water Policy and Supply, Division of Shell Fisheries, Division of Fish and Game, Public Shooting and Fishing, Division of Veterans Services, State Rent Control Office, and finally debt service on the bonds issued by the division. It contains also the Bureau of Aeronautics, Bureau of Commerce, Bureau of Forests, Parks and Historic Sights, Bureau of Geology and Topography, Bureau of Housing, Bureau of Navigation, and the Bureau of Recreation.

The most important function of the division should be the planning of the orderly development of the state. Unfortunately little has been accomplished in this area. The most recent Development Plan for New Jersey was published in 1950, and even this was only 33 pages long. The Governor and the legislature do not know what is going to happen in the state and have made little preparation for its growth and development. Certainly there should be one agency that anticipates the growth of government, makes suggestion for the orderly development of plans in the state to meet the recreation, the highway, the water needs, and the needs resulting from the growth of commerce in New Jersey. Not least, the requirements of the Bureau of Commerce suggest that, if New Jersey is to grow, something more should be invested in making plant sites known to prospective firms and in promotional advertising to make better known the advantages of location in New Jersey.

The difficulties of finding such funds are again a reflection of the failure of the state revenue system to provide an adequate budget for the planning function. A few individuals are working against the greatest odds in an attempt to plan for the state but they are constantly being diverted by other demands upon their time. Most of the future developments in the state can be anticipated. If constant revision was expected, there would be few areas in which events to come could not be planned and the necessary financial adjustments made in the state budget. Many of the excess costs that the state will have to face could have been avoided if more attention had been devoted to the planning function in past years. The highway requirements, the needs of schools, the need for parks and other recreational facilities, the higher education requirements, the need for better staff and personnel, and finally the need for a better revenue system could all have been anticipated had the planning function been better done.

Unfortunately the efforts of those candidates for office who had recognized this need were not effective since they had pledged themselves against a sales or income tax. Tradition is a powerful instrument, but had there been planning nothing could have prevented a forward look in state politics. As a matter of fact for a man to win an election a considerable number of people must change their vote from the party of their first choice to the opposition candidate. So long as this is true there will be a danger that both parties will stay on the overconservative side. Once the state faces reality, such efforts to becloud the issues will no longer be successful, but it is my fear that it will be many years before reality is faced.

There is a general shortage of staff throughout the Division of Conservation and Economic Development. For example, the immediate water needs of the state are to be taken care of by the acquisition of Round Valley and Spruce Run reservoirs. But no one knows where the next reservoir will be placed nor has the land for it been acquired. The recent bond issue authorizing Round Valley did provide funds for a study of water resources. This study ought to be made at once, for the longer the delay the more costly will the land become. In too many instances the land will be acquired only if there is extensive condemnation of existing buildings and other rights. Certainly it is not too much to ask that the state spend some money now to save a larger sum later. Only as advance planning is done can the state avoid unnecessary expense. There is no excuse for the current policy of neglect of the planning functions.

Another example of neglect of the promotional activities of the state is found in the Bureau of Commerce. In this case available funds are completely inadequate. The resort business has been neglected. The advertising functions also are neglect-ed as are the inducements to attract industry to the state. In many states the corresponding bureau will locate industrial property, and in some of the southern states will even build a plant and lease it to the prospective tenant. The fact is that the entire effort in New Jersey is on a superficial basis and inade-quately supported. Practically no research work is being done at the present time, and the ability to follow up on new leads and prospects is notable for its absence. Even the building division is found in this department, but there is no staff to do the work. Still another helpful activity would be the development of export and import services to attract certain types of industry to the state, but again there is no one to do the job. Most of the infor-mation that the bureau acquires about the location of new indus-try in the state is the result of reports from the Department of Labor and Industry. In each case the character of the reports leaves much to be desired, and the reports are often late in ar-riving. It is clear that if New Jersey were not so strategically located the failure of this bureau to do its job would have cost the state much more than any expenditure for its promotion.

In other areas the same complaint is found. The veterans' loan organization that issued many million dollars' worth of loans after the war finds that it has lost so much of its person-nel that it cannot begin to keep track of the individuals with whom it should be in constant contact. Although the Attorney General is to take over the servicing of these loans, there will be losses in the record of borrowers that could have been avoid-ed had there been an adequate staff to keep the individuals under constant contact with the loan authorities.

In the Division of Shell Fisheries the same story prevails. There are too few individuals and too few boats to enforce the law. There are now approximately thirty persons on patrol of the shellfish areas. If there were at least some sixty, a more adequate job could be done. As things are now, the individuals who wish to steal shellfish know exactly where all the men of the force are at almost any time. With more and better boats a better job could be done and the laws of the state properly en-forced. In view of the growing shortage of shellfish a more ade-quate control of the beds would protect a valuable asset and the livelihood of many workers. Here again the penny-wise and pound-foolish policy has prevailed. It is of interest to note, however, that the shellfish experts are enthusiastic about pol-luted areas. The oysters in such areas are not fit to eat, but it does not prevent their propagation of new beds. Once the spawn have left the polluted area none of the contamination remains and the new oyster is as healthy as the waters in which he is found.

The Division of Fish and Game and the Division of Public Shooting and Fishing find that many of the most valuable assets of the state have been polluted to a point at which few if any fish can survive. Again it is a foolish policy, in a state as densely settled as New Jersey, not to impose rigid restrictions on the possibility of pollution and to protect the few streams that can give so much recreation to the people of the state. One of the state's greatest assets is the Delaware River, but below Trenton it has been polluted to the danger point. The various towns along its banks have been dumping their sewage into it and thus have made one of the most attractive rivers unfit for either fish or swimming. New parks have not been created along the river, almost entirely neglecting one of the greatest assets of the state. Even existing parks have not been developed to the point of real recreational advantage to the people.

This leads into a discussion of the general park situation in New Jersey. The state is the proud possessor of Island Beach, but little development of this attractive stretch of dunes has been attempted. What is required is a causeway across the bay to give access by automobiles. Actually the state has not decided what should be done with the beach. Recently some limited use of the beach has been permitted to parties who first received permission from the state authorities. But this waste of one of the best stretches of undeveloped land in the state has been due to the lack of funds. Money needs to be found to build the highway that will give access to one of the truly great recreational areas in the state's possession.

Other possibilities include the opening of reservoirs and private lakes to public fishing, the purchase of access points to lakes and larger rivers, the building of docks and boat-launching facilities on the larger lakes and rivers, the running of boat liveries where private enterprise cannot undertake the job, the proper management of our larger rivers, such as the Delaware, Raritan, Hackensack, Passaic, Wading, and Great Egg Harbor, and of our estuaries. All in all the state has done a poor job of providing the sort of recreation needed by its people.

But the real problem is the shortage of play space in the congested areas and the neglect of those now in use. Particularly in Northeast New Jersey there are inadequate public parks and inadequate recreational facilities. Unfortunately, to acquire the necessary land at this late date would involve public expend-itures far exceeding those that would have been required even a few years ago. In 1950 New Jersey had only 129,907 acres of state-owned land devoted to forests, parks, and fish and game preserves, a ratio of 26 acres per thousand people. Since that date the state has acquired another 181,461 acres for public recreation. Thus at the present time the state owns 311,368 acres of land for public use. Since 1950 the population also has risen, and the ratio of public parks and other recreational areas in relation to the population now amounts to 31.2 acres per thousand population, which is a more favorable figure than that of 1950-51, but is not nearly enough.

The latest report by the Committee on Parks and Public Lands was issued in July, 1941. It was prepared for and ap-proved by the New Jersey State Planning Board and given the title *A Parks and Public Lands Program for New Jersey*. All the quotations that follow have been taken from this report and the page is indicated in parentheses at the end of each quotation:

"New Jersey is in both relative and absolute need of addi-tional outdoor recreational facilities of all kinds. Its munici-palities and counties have less than a third of the needed park and playground lands, and the greatest deficiencies are found in areas of greatest congestion and greatest need. The State has less than a tenth as much state park, forest, and other such public lands, per capita, as now provided by New York and Pennsylvania . . . " (1)

"Hundreds of thousands of acres of land useful for recrea-tional and other public purposes are now worse than wasted. This land has no prospect of profitable private use. Much of it is chronically tax delinquent and imposes a severe financial burden upon many of the rural townships. Planned and syste-matic transfer of large areas of such land from private to State ownership will at one and the same time benefit the State, give important financial relief to the townships, and turn these lands from steady deterioration to increasing public usefulness." (2)

"The State's streams and other waterways and public high-ways are subject to continuous spoilation due to lack of reason-able regulations to be exercised by the localities and the State. These regulations cost little and when properly applied would result in mutual benefit to both land owners and the public." (3)

"No streams or other inland waters close within the urban areas of the State, are clean enough for swimming or most other recreational uses. Many streams even in rural districts are shamefully littered with trash and some are too polluted to be of much recreational value. Cities of the State are being forced farther and farther afield for potable water. Little has been done to make accessible to the public those streams and waters still usable for recreational purposes." (4)

Various proposals are made in the report for the acquisition of additional ocean-front parks, the development of Hackensack Meadows for recreational use, and the importance of stream improvement. Not all of the program can be completed within a few years, but there should be a plan for the steady development of recreational areas in the state and the establishment of a large-enough budget so that much of the land can be acquired within a relatively few years. Any such plan will cost money, of course, but if New Jersey is to prosper it must spend the needed money to assure its people sufficient recreational opportunity.

Still another matter that is bound to come to the attention of the public is the need for urban renewal in the major areas of the state. Trenton, Newark, Hudson County, Elizabeth, Perth Amboy, and other industrial centers will deteriorate unless some greater effort is made to prevent their decline. In the end it will probably come to the need for subsidization of public housing and the development of more recreational areas at great expense to the municipality and the state. The problem arises from the tendency for the wealthier families to move into the city. So long as this trend continues there will be overcrowding and high rents, and delinquency will grow apace in the congested centers. Most of the individuals affected cannot afford to pay the rents demanded for living decently in the center of a city.

Slums cost thousands of dollars more for police, for fire protection, and for the necessary recreation that is the only means of offsetting the trend toward delinquency. There is no easy solution, but if the cities are not to decline and become festering sores bringing disgrace to the State, some effort will have to be made to overcome these difficulties. Not least important are the values represented by real estate in the central cities. No one will want to see these values decline, but decline they will unless the cities and the state make some early effort to prevent the growth of generally deteriorating neighborhoods and real slums.

A serious problem is posed by the growth of communities that are poorly built with box-type houses. There is real danger that many of these communities will become rural slums when the original purchasers depart and less and less desirable tenants move in. Like so many problems this one is easy to solve, but an effort must be made to avoid the necessity. The number of such areas in New Jersey is large, and vigilance is called for if we are to prevent such developments.

In concluding this chapter we re-emphasize the need for planning. Until adequate studies and plans are made and kept up to date neither the Governor nor the legislature can anticipate the needs of the state and all will tend to operate on a hand-to-mouth basis. Planning takes money, and so long as the state is short of funds there will be insufficient money for an adequate job. The real question is whether the legislature would appropriate adequate funds to prepare a complete plan for the development of the state into the years of growth that will be characteristic of New Jersey in the future. At the present time there seems to be little interest in doing more than getting by for another year. Even in the General Assembly there is little chance of finding the sort of leadership required at the present time.

Much could be done by vigorous action, but until state officials are willing to act the people are not likely to be properly informed about the deficiencies of the state and the need for a completely revised tax and revenue system. Certainly the growing requirements are not going to be met by further increases in the level of the general property tax. As already indicated, reaction against the property tax has begun and little more can be expected from this source.

Finding the necessary leadership in New Jersey has been a matter of concern for a long time. Yet if the state is not to decline there must be leadership. Two of the greatest barriers to progress have been the operations of some representatives of the press and some of the leaders of commerce, business, and finance. In their efforts to keep a low tax rate neither group has given adequate thought to the requirements of the public. Yet it is the provision of good services that will keep the state a vigorous and progressive community, and investments for education, recreation, and planning will make New Jersey a better state to live in. Other needs appear in the field of institutions and agencies, where a small investment might make possible the return of many individuals to a more productive role in the community. Custodial care is a poor way of making provision for the sick.

It is the peculiar characteristics of New Jersey that make

leadership so difficult to achieve. Too many individuals are primarily involved in their business interests in New York or Philadelphia and take little interest in the affairs of the state. Too many read the New York and Philadelphia papers only. Too few take an active interest in public affairs.

It is the Governor who must provide leadership. Unless he is willing to risk his political future, little will be done. Many devices are available which would permit him to make a dramatic appeal to the citizens of the state. One would be to indicate the extent of the deficits that now exist. Another would be to appoint lay boards to make a real investigation of the needs of the state in all important areas. Still another device would be that of calling in experts to make surveys of these needs. Any one of these devices would prove that New Jersey will decline unless more is spent for the management of public affairs and for the people of the state.

CHAPTER V

Department of Institutions
and Agencies

The gravest problem of the Department of Institutions and Agencies is the inability to get enough revenue to support the program to which they are committed. The problem arises from the lack of an adequate revenue system and the need to pay more to get qualified people and to train the personnel they already have.

Another problem of the department is that it has had to live with the independent boards that have control of its entire operations. There are also boards that have tended to gain a proprietary interest in each of the institutions with which they are connected. This has led to some differences of opinion about personnel. There are occasions when a board can be of considerable help to the department, but on the whole the boards have not been of as much help as they should in arousing public interest for the sake of providing more adequate medical care for those who are in mental institutions and in other hospitals.

The first indictment of the department is found in the ratio of psychiatrists to patients. Table IV indicates this ratio in the various mental institutions of the state.

TABLE IV

PSYCHIATRISTS IN RELATION TO PATIENTS[1]
FISCAL YEAR 1957

Trenton	1 psychiatrist to each 344.9 patients
Greystone Park	1 psychiatrist to each 548.7 patients
Marlboro	1 psychiatrist to each 591.6 patients
Ancora	1 psychiatrist to each 375.17 patients
Neuro-Psychiatric Institute	1 psychiatrist to each 191 patients
Brisbane	No psychiatrist

1. State of New Jersey, Department of Institutions and Agencies, Bureau of Social Research, *Summary Statistical Report—Fiscal Year 1957.*

The number of physicians is also inadequate. The care we should give to our patients requires a larger number of physicians. Table V indicates the ratio of physicians to patients in each of the State institutions.

TABLE V

PHYSICIANS IN RELATION TO PATIENTS[2]
FISCAL YEAR 1957

Trenton	1 physician to each 128 patients
Greystone Park	1 physician to each 171.43 patients
Marlboro	1 physician to each 155.68 patients
Ancora	1 physician to each 132.41 patients
Neuro-Psychiatric Institute	1 physician to each 106 patients
Brisbane	1 physician to each 93 patients

A similar pattern is followed with regard to the number of psychologists to patients. Table VI suggests that this figure is just as bad as that found in the other categories.

TABLE VI

PSYCHOLOGISTS IN RELATION TO EACH PATIENT[3]

Trenton	1 psychologist to each 481 patients
Greystone Park	1 psychologist to each 548.7 patients
Marlboro	1 psychologist to each 591.6 patients
Ancora	1 psychologist to each 750.33 patients
Neuro-Psychiatric Institute	1 psychologist to each 191 patients
Brisbane	1 psychologist to each 43 patients

The number of nurses ranges from one to as many as 39.19 patients at Greystone Park to a low of one nurse to each 5.75 patients at Ancora. Why there should be this discrepancy is hard to fathom, but the ratio suggests that there is a wide dif-

2. *Ibid.*
3. *Ibid.*

ference in the quality of the care received in various institutions over the state.

All this compares unfavorably with the practice found in other states of comparable wealth. The following states have substantially better ratios of psychiatrists to patients than is found in New Jersey: Delaware a ratio of 231 patients to each psychiatrist; Idaho with a ratio of 306 patients to each psychiatrist; Kansas with a ratio of 316 patients to each psychiatrist; Maine with a ratio of 273 patients to each psychiatrist; and finally Hawaii with a ratio of 304 patients to each psychaitrist.

The position with regard to physicians is much worse, as revealed by the following figures: Kansas leads with a ratio of one physician to 56 patients; Delaware is next with a ratio of one physician to 107 patients. On the whole it is fair to state that New Jersey is close to the bottom of the list of states that care for their patients in state institutions. The crime is that many of these individuals could be returned to society if given the proper medical care. There is no reason for neglecting these people who are too sick to care for themselves or too poor to pay their bills.

The problem of mental health is not one that will diminish over the years. There are a great many patients who should be given more than merely custodial care; an effort should be made to restore their health so that they may again become productive members of society instead of being dependent upon the state. There is no reason for our failure to give them the sort of care provided by modern medicine. Naturally many individuals in state institutions are of advanced age and need custodial state care until they die, since otherwise they would place an enormous burden upon their families. And the number of these old people will increase as medicine lengthens the life span. Therefore, if we do not wish to double the size and number of our state hospitals, there must be a much greater effort to cure those who can be cured.

The weakness of the current program in New Jersey is revealed by the following suggestions made by the American Psychiatric Association: that to provide adequate care there should be 107 more physicians than are now employed by the state; that there should be 15 more psychiatrists than are now employed; and there should be 1,140 more nurses. This is indeed a severe indictment of present standards in the hospitals of the state. In spite of the fact that there are so few nurses, New Jersey stands twelfth from the bottom among the states. This suggests that there are other laggards as well.

The Lay Boards

An excellent suggestion has been made by one of the group engaged in the study of our state hospitals over the past year. This is that the power of the boards over personnel should be abolished, and the boards should be required to report annually to the Governor on the standards that prevail in the state hospitals. This would serve to call to the attention of the voting public the neglect of these hospitals and the need to raise the standards in them. It would also serve to dramatize the needs of the hospitals and to create a vocal minority in favor of doing much more than is now done. Such reports should be set forth in simple terms and with the minimum of psychiatric terminology. What the state needs is a clear statement of the level of operation required to give more than mere custodial care to the patients in our hospitals. Given this knowledge, the people would soon develop a much greater interest. There is no assurance that this will be the case so long as the revenue system proves inadequate, but there should develop over the years, a much greater concern about conditions in such institutions. Knowing the quality of men and women who serve on the lay boards, there is no question but that they could arouse considerable support for doing a much better job.

Little will be done until the revenue of the state has been raised to the point where it can support an adequate program of care of the mental patients and others in the hospitals of the state. Until then there is little chance that we will be able to raise the standards of the state institutions or give the inmates the sort of care that is required by modern medical standards.

Division of Correction and Parole

"It is a well known fact that probation services in New Jersey range from among the best to among the worst in the United States. A report of the National Probation and Parole Association to the Law Enforcement Council made in 1955 highlights the problems of New Jersey in this area."[4]

---

4. *The Future of Correction in New Jersey,* Department of Institutions and Agencies, Division of Correction and Parole, F. Lovell Bixby, Director, p. 1. (Mimeograph.) The following quotations are from this source with the page reference appearing at the end of each.

"In view of the problems that arise in this area, there are many reasons to advocate the development of a Probation Coordinator who would have only advisory powers to recommend standards, to assist in procuring and training personnel, and to maintain State-wide statistics. The reason for this recommendation is the strongly entrenched traditions of local autonomy in our county courts. The division of Correction and Parole has consistently advocated the latter course as the most practical first step. Also, because of the manifest fear of Institutions and Agencies 'encroachment,' the Department has refrained from taking a strong public position on probation matters." (2)

There is also the possibility of the State Board of Control wanting to advocate more radically improved probation services —which means some sort of centralized supervision and control —on the basis that the institutional and parole loads might be greatly reduced by the increased use of probation. "If such a decision is reached, the Division of Correction and Parole strongly recommends that the Court Administrator's office rather than Institutions and Agencies be given the responsibility for the care of probation cases. Probation should be an arm of the courts. Courts in our culture have a position of great strength. The result is often to leave the probation and parole services combined, thus parole suffers the fictional fate of the step-child." (3)

One other need is evident. This is the need for much more attention to "diagnostic procedures, residential group centers, specialized group centers, specialized facilities for defective delinquents and borderline psychotics, and minimum security camps. While some institutional building will be necessary, need for more maximum security is not apparent in the foreseeable future." (3) "The term 'correctional institution' should be used in place of the term 'reformatory' with a specific thought in mind. Prisons, penitentiaries, and reformatories have certain traditional and legal significances which interfere with their flexible use to meet changing problems." (5)

The Bureau of Social Research indicates the following needs by the year 1975 (6): Refer to table on top of page 46.

"Based upon past experience, of the estimated 515 commitments approximately 100 will classify as defective delinquents. It would seem desirable that suitable facilities be provided in a mental deficiency institution for this group. The law now makes New Lisbon responsible for defective delinquents, but no facilities equal to the task have been provided." (2)

Age	Estimated Number of Commitments	Estimated Commitments by Classification		Average Stay in Months	Gross Beds Needed
		Male	Female		
8-12	115	115	10		0
13, 14, 15	515	Jamesburg	515	12	515
16-20	1,490	Annandale	1048	12	1,048
		Bordentown	363	24	726
		Prison	79	20	142
21-30	1,100	495 (Med) New		24	990
		605 Prison Leesburg Farm		20	1,089
31+	505	505 Prison Rahway Farm		20	909

"It is also true that the deficiencies of the century-old Trenton Prison as the main penal institution of the State are too well known to need elaboration. However, it would seem most unwise for New Jersey to incur the expense of a maximum security bastille for the relatively few who require that degree of security.

"It is recommended therefore, that the present prison be retained and remodeled to serve as a receiving and classification unit for all prison commitments. It would also serve as the 'collecting point' for men being picked up on writs and detainers.

"Such a plan is contingent upon building a modern, medium security industrial prison at some location outside of Trenton. There seem to be many arguments in favor of locating it on the same reservation as the Leesburg Farm." (7 and 8)

An alternate plan would be to develop more and better local facilities with the Diagnostic Center serving increasingly as a recourse for only the more difficult, complicated problems. Of these alternatives, the latter seems by far the wiser, although the construction of a second center is probably inevitable before 1975.

Sex Offenders

"The diagnostic and parole procedures established by special legislation for sex offenders are working well. But the use of

State hospitals leaves much to be desired. For the most part, the staff of these institutions have so many worries that the pressure of these non-psychotics is an additional, different, and unwelcome problem." (11)

"All of the hospitals have accepted the burden and done their best. It might be, however, that a special unit—perhaps at the New Jersey Neuro-Psychiatric Institute—would be the best way to add more treatment to the rest of the program for this class of offender. Although not specifically referred to in the New Jersey Neuro-Psychiatric Institute Law, sex offenders are of a class with drug addicts and alcoholics who are mentioned in the law." (11)

Parole

"The future problems of parole are largely a matter of keeping up with an expanding case load. The present case load is 3851. The case load by 1975 will be 5186 or a projected increase of 1335." (12) This suggests that the present staff will need at least seventy additional persons qualified to deal with parole problems. We should also experiment with the California plan of intensive supervision by especially skilled officers during the first few months of parole when most failures occur. We should also experiment with guided interaction (group therapy) for parolees in the larger population centers.

Personnel Policies

"Some time ago the writer was inquiring why one cell block in a Federal Penitentiary has a huge enrollment in evening school, while a similar cell block had no men going to school. The answer came from a prisoner who said, 'If a guy comes along with a book and asks if you want to go to school and another guy with a club tells you to forget it and stay in your cell —what can you do?'" (5)

The area of officer discipline has been and continues to be bothersome under the present system of Civil Service hearings. The difficulties do not ordinarily involve questions of guilt or innocence. Too often the appointing authority is embarrassed by having its decision as to the penalty for infractions overruled or modified by The Civil Service Commission. The Federal Prison Bureau has solved this problem, with the cooperation of the Federal Civil Service, by setting up a standardized schedule of minimum and maximum punishments for common infractions.

"All recruitment, therefore, should provide an initial period of paid trainee status before achieving regular appointment in grade, and completion of advanced professional studies should be recognized by extra salary increments." (5)

What is clearly needed is the growth of the morale of the staff that is in charge of the prisoners, parole officers and others who have to work with those who have some part of the job of providing for work with offenders. Advanced standing for those who have worked hard at their jobs should be the least recognition accorded to any one of those persons. Eagerness to improve should be fostered as a way of raising morale. Not least, those who have failed should be discharged without serious qualms, since the morale of the parolee or prisoner is to be encouraged as much as possible.

Little can be accomplished, however, so long as those in charge cannot enforce discipline and cannot get rid of subordinates who fail to perform adequately. Discipline must be restored and the officers of each institution empowered to use methods that can and will work.

Public Assistance

The State of New Jersey should be forever ashamed of the low level of public assistance that is offered its citizens. In 1957 the state was third from the bottom in per capita expenditures for public assistance. This is a reflection upon the state not only because it is wealthy, but also because there are high concentrations of urban populations with a greater than normal need for public assistance. Again the problem is that of finding the revenue to finance a more adequate program.

This is due in part to the emphasis upon local autonomy and in part to the lack of an adequate state revenue system. The share paid by most counties is well above that demanded in most states and beyond the average that prevails over the entire United States. What is needed is the presentation of an adequate plan for financing the requirements by the state and the sharing of the benefits on the basis of need, so that those who require assistance can get it as they need it.

In the three categories of aid to the aged, aid to dependent children, and aid to the blind there is an unusually low supplement from the state to increase the benefits payable. The financing of these aids in New Jersey is considerably more difficult than in most states of equal wealth.

The state needs a whole series of diagnostic centers, relief agencies, and other institutions capable of taking care of those who are either lacking the intelligence to work effectively or are in desperate need of relief. There is no substitute for money, and so long as New Jersey continues to stress economy at whatever price conditions will remain the same.

As has been indicated, too little effort is made to care for the needy in New Jersey. Little is done in the hospitals, little is done for those on parole, little is done for those who need relief or are deserving of public assistance. So long as these conditions continue many people in this state will lack adequate food and adequate housing. This should not happen in a state as wealthy as New Jersey.

A new attitude must be developed if the state is to do what it should for those unfortunate enough to require public assistance or the benefits of the hospitals, the parole boards, or even the tuberculosis sanitariums. We should hang our heads in shame over the present low level of public assistance. But how to generate this attitude is the question that should be uppermost in everyone's mind. So long as the insistence on no new taxes continues there can be no change. There seems to be scant liberal leadership in the state. How this can be formulated is the question. Current levels of assistance, health, and diagnostic centers are so low that even some of the poorer states will exceed the performance found in New Jersey.

Prison Industries

Little thought has been given to the rehabilitation of the men confined in our prisons. These men should be taught skills so that when they are released they can pursue some useful employment. "Rehabilitation programs represent the attempt to overcome the evils of idleness. An idle prisoner is more difficult to care for than one who is employed. Abhorring complete inactivity, he utilizes his time to cultivate bitterness and concoct further crime, awaiting only the opportunity to enact it. As a result prison terms are lengthened through the avoidance of early parole, the rate of return to prison is accelerated, and the over-all cost to society tends upward."[5]

5. *Improving State Use Industries,* New Jersey Taxpayers Association, p. 1. The following quotations are from this source with the page reference appearing at the end of each.

"The second great responsibility of a prison, therefore, is to
provide a program of rehabilitation. Such a program is essen-
tially a program of activity. But more activity will not suffice.
It must have meaning; it must lead somewhere. It must generate helpful attitudes and provide useful skills and so prepare
the prisoner to assume the normal responsibilities of citizen-
ship as imposed by life under today's highly industrialized conditions. Thus the objectives of training and production cannot
and should not be divorced." (1)

"Prison industries meet these criteria. The prisoner is set
to work actually producing something that has value both in
training and in use." (1)

"New opportunities for diversified prisoner employment may
well develop from the use of new materials and techniques. En-
try into such additional fields should be guided by (1) stability
of product demand, (2) avoidance of operations requiring equipment subject to rapid obsolescence and (3) emphasis on industries in which the labor content is high and capital investment
is low. Specifically, it is recommended that the State Use Industries explore the following possibilities: Synthetic Fabric
Weaving, Book Repair, Meat Cutting, Salvage, Metal Furniture
Making, Paint Manufacture, and Expansion of Canning Operations Using Frozen or Southern Grown Fruit and Vegetables." (3)

"State Use Industries should continue its policy of manufacturing only those items in which it can bring its prices at least
in line with the open market for products of comparable quality.
Such prices should reflect the full cost of products, including
any costs of transportation borne by using institutions. Moreover, this policy should be reiterated periodically in Bureau
communications." (4)

"The Bureau of State Use Industries can and should be self-
supporting, but long-standing State policies and actions in di-
verting Bureau funds have rendered it incapable of meeting its
immediate financial problems and giving gainful employment to
all idle prisoners. It is in the public interest, and a matter of
economy, that this situation be remedied. But this cannot be
done unless the Bureau is given help in overcoming in a small
way the deficiencies which have developed because the State, to
the detriment of the prison system, has utilized a large share of
past earnings." (6)

"Useful goods and articles are manufactured in the work
program under the brand name of 'SUDIA' (State Use Department of Institutions and Agencies) and are sold to tax supported

institutions, agencies and subdivisions of the State. The market is limited by law to such customers and the latter may not purchase from another source without consent of the Bureau." (9)

"During the course of the survey, it was indicated that, while most instructors are capable, this is not uniformly so; also that Civil Service requirements seem to make it unduly difficult to enforce high standards of performance or to replace a supervisor whose services are unsatisfactory. Whatever the difficulty, Civil Service requirements for supplying personnel under an equitable system of employment should permit the maintaining of high standards of production and quality of instruction while still providing adequate safeguards for employees." (17)

"State Use Industries should make optimum use of available products testing facilities, including: (1) the testing, specifications and inspection section in the Bureau of Purchase, (2) available resources of other state agencies, and (3) services of outside agencies where necessary. Findings should be made known only to SUDIA customs, identifying the competitive products solely by number or letter designation." (26)

Still another question is the question of style. Every SUDIA item may be said to have style, but the question is: does the style appeal to the customer?

It is the current view of the bureau that State Use Industries should not add to the cost of its products by adding qualities which do not increase the service life. On the other hand, few commercial products today are immune from some degree of styling. Furthermore, if style has served to increase sales of commercial goods, it should have a similar effect on the sales of SUDIA products.

The bureau has a major interest in clothing for patients and inmates of state and county hospitals and correctional institutions, where morale plays a large role in cure and rehabilitation. "Good morale stems from self respect. Clothing plays a part in this process and when institutional clothing is overly standardized it inhibits rather than helps early cures. Style variety in furniture, curtains, bed spreads and other items is also important, since it contributes to making a hospital less forbidding and more livable." (27)

"In correctional units also, variety and style of clothing can be used effectively to reward achievement and improve morale. At Clinton Reformatory for Women, an unfenced honor institution, the girls who progress most rapidly are permitted to wear more attractive dresses and colors, while others must be content with the ordinary run of institutional clothing with its monotonous uniformity and frequent ill fit.'' (17)

State Use Industries needs a warehousing and distribution system to make its goods available to the various consumers. The report previously mentioned has suggested that Fernwood Warehouse be used for this purpose. It should be possible for State Use Industries to ship goods promptly to those who want them. There is no substitute for a warehouse where goods can be stored and then shipped on demand. (31)

Quality Control

"Random or 'statistical' inspection might be adequate to keep most rejectable SUDIA products within reasonable percentages. While some products may require 100 per cent inspection to assure safety and high dependability in service, even the canning of fruits and vegetables at Annandale and Leesburg (operations involving the safety of the consumer) might be susceptible to adequate statistical inspection. A guide is available in the practice of established commercial canneries.'' (35)

"It is believed that the Bureau's attempt to achieve high quality in its products would be greatly strengthened by independent or semi-independent inspection which would formally establish the extent to which quality standards are being met.'' (35)

The great advantage of the SUDIA industries is that they would achieve the end that most citizens of the state desire--the rehabilitation of a high percentage of prisoners to useful employment.

A real need of the prison system is for more minimum-security type institutions. Farms, labor camps, and park buildings are needed so that the prisoner will not be confined within walls and can serve a useful existence without the maximum restraint.

Further, much more attention should be paid to the juvenile offender. Many of them can be salvaged if they are given the required attention by skilled persons. Many of these offenders need not be placed in institutions labeled as reformatories or in prisons. Much could be done along this line if the finances were available. Menlo Park ought to be expanded but so far the needs of this institution have been grossly neglected.

Relief and Welfare

The inadequacy of the relief and welfare programs of the state has already been cited. These programs should be greatly expanded in order to offer fuller service to those citizens who are in real need and have only the state to look to for help. One difficulty lies in the fact that the calls for relief rise during a depression while the revenues of the state tend to decline at the same time. Therefore, much of what should be done is left to the private charitable institutions or the local relief agencies. One answer to this problem lies in the use of federal funds. The government could help by grants based upon need in the event that local relief needs exceeded the state's ability to finance them, but few states would like to become dependent upon the federal government for such handouts.

Analysis of Waiting List, Institutions for the Mentally Deficient

As of April 30, 1958, there were 609 children waiting to be admitted into homes for the mentally deficient. The needs of these children had been certified by state authorities and their admission was urgently desired. Yet there are still too few places for the care of those suffering from this form of mental illness.

Admissions from the community during fiscal year 1959 leaped from the 346 reported the previous year to a total of 538. This increased rate of admissions will continue, because of the larger population from which to draw the mentally deficient.

Mental Hygiene

The few mental hygiene clinics that now exist in the state are financed by a grant of 20 cents per capita. In New York the state aid amounts to $1 per capita, five times the money available in New Jersey. If more money were made available, many of the patients could be referred to the mental hygiene clinics for treatment before they became psychotic.

Conclusions

There is little need to point up the deficiencies in the support of the Department of Institutions and Agencies. Too little is spent to do an adequate job in any of the areas that they attempt to work in, and our state hospitals form one of the primary areas of neglect. There is nothing that a better job of revenue collection could not solve; but the failure of the state in this area has resulted both in inadequate relief and welfare benefits and in poor care for the mentally deficient.

CHAPTER VI
Other Departments in State Government

Secretary of State

In this department the work is of a routine nature, though many of the employees need experience. The Bingo Commission is doing a good job, as is the Athletic Commission. There seems to be little need for either additional personnel or major changes in this department.

Civil Service

This is the primary procurement agency of the state government. It also includes many municipal governments. The basic problem is that this department has had a high rate of turnover, which has led to difficulties.

There are not enough sharp minds in the civil service to check the requesting agencies on job requirements. Also there has been a tendency to uphold the employee in almost every case. This point was made in the discussion on prisons and is true of too many other parts of the state system.

Banking and Insurance

The problem here is that the personnel requirements cannot be met under existing salary schedule. There is great need for more actuaries, more field men, and for men to take care of small loans. In the matter of savings and loan funds there is need for more men of quality.

In addition there is need for more men to supervise the cemeteries. The people who buy perpetual care for their plots should be assured that their payments will be properly used.

In the consumer credit field there is need for a much larger staff and the addition of better qualified people. There is also need for more clerks at the minimum level. The field of banking is well taken care of at the present time.

The rise in the state civil service salary schedule may permit some of these needs to be met by an increase in the salaries paid to many of those under civil service. The question is the beginning salary to be paid those who are seeking jobs. If these salaries are low there will be few applicants. If they are high there will be a great improvement in the personnel quality of the Banking and Insurance Department.

The unfortunate fact is that at the present time the department cannot police the law.

Agriculture

There are few well-qualified people in the department at the present time. As already indicated, the salaries paid to workers in the agricultural field are well below those paid to others in state employment.

The milk industry is under federal control, so this does not present a problem.

Defense

This field includes the administration of national defense, national guard, and naval militia. One of the biggest problems is that those who work for the military get more than those who work for the state.

Little has been done to bring civil defense up to the level that might be required if we were attacked. A grand total of $95,000 is annually appropriated for this purpose.

Public Utilities

In this field there is a general weakness of staff and not enough depth. More money should be spent to raise the level of competence of the staff so that they will prove equal to the task set before them. Again there is hope that the new pay scale will prove advantageous to this agency.

Health

At the present time this department is doing a good job. But too much time is spent at conferences.

Labor

The primary difficulty here is that the department is tied in too closely with the labor movement.

It is true also that this department is inefficient and the great need is for the adoption of more modern machine methods.

There is also a tendency for the workmen's compensation to be too liberal and for the rehabilitation commission to go overboard in doing favorable things for people.

Highway Department

The greatest present need here is for better-qualified engineers. In many cases outside engineers are hired to obtain a higher level of competence.

We also face a serious problem in the field of rapid transit. This raises the question of the need for some sort of subsidy to make the rapid transit system work. There will be many objections to this but it would be a lot cheaper than the building of roads and the burden this would place on the state.

Law and Public Safety

DIVISION OF MOTOR VEHICLES

This division needs many more people for enforcement, and there are not enough inspectors for the new drivers' applications that arise each year.

STATE POLICE

The New Jersey State Police are better staffed and equipped than in most other states of comparable character and need little more money.

ALCOHOLIC BEVERAGE CONTROL

At the present time these people are doing a good job and need little more money or staff.

TENEMENT HOUSING

In this field there is need to do much more than is being done at the present time. One of these days there may be a major disaster and the state will realize that it has not been living up to its responsibilities. Many inspectors should be added to the staff of the tenement house division and the quality of their work should be raised.

LAW

There should be more persons in this division and they should be better paid. The constitutional revision greatly improved the quality of our courts, but if there is no possibility of getting the best-qualified people into them a general deterioration in the administration of justice will result.

TRAFFIC SAFETY

More will be done here as the result of the new campaign to enforce the law and to take away the licenses of those drivers who have violated the law too many times. The use of the test for alcoholism also is a step forward.

TREASURY

The administrative division is in good shape.

However in budget and accounting there is need for more men of quality and more pay for those who now work in this field.

TAXATION

A better staff would result in the possibility of raising more revenue.

There should be more people in the field of the corporation tax.

It is true also that more people could be used in the collection of death duties.

One tax problem is that the equalized values in real estate do not represent enough cases to make a fair judgment. This is an important area as the amount of state aid for education is based upon the equalized valuations as determined by the department of taxation.

LOCAL GOVERNMENT

The basic issue here is that government has been centralized in Trenton so that there is a tendency to look to Trenton for advice. The problem is that the quality of the individuals concerned with stale government is not too far above the quality of those engaged in the administration of the local governments.

Consolidation of local districts, more attention to the relief needs of local governments, more effort to merge various townships and boroughs would be helpful. Of course there are many reasons why most townships and boroughs do not want to consolidate, the main one being the differential in the tax rate between one area and another.

TAX APPEALS

The result of the tradition against tax appeals has been to deny many citizens the right to justice. The Sixth Report of the New Jersey Commission on State Tax Policy pointed out the vast differences in the assessment practices in different parts of the state. On the whole, a declining property is assessed at a higher percentage of true value than is a prosperous property. Business property tends to be assessed at a higher percentage of true value than residential property. The most extreme case is found in Hudson County, where business property is assessed at almost twice the value of residential property.

What is to be done about this state of affairs? The Sixth Report, just mentioned, suggested a move to a county assessment basis. In view of the quality of the freeholders who are elected, this raises a real question. Perhaps it would be better to centralize the entire administration at the level of the Department of Taxation and appoint the assessors at that level. The chance of getting well-qualified assessors would be greatly enhanced if this were done. Local politics would not enter into the decision and an appropriate examination could be held, under the Civil Service Commission. The real issue is that of getting the best-qualified assessors to do the job. There can be little improvement until this has been done.

RACING COMMISSION

So far as anyone can tell, this agency has been doing a reasonably good job.

DIVISION OF INVESTMENT

In this area there is real need for at least two more good security analysts. The addition of such persons would add greatly to the quality of the investment decisions made and would improve the rate of return realized by this division.

PENSIONS

This is an area in which the state has taken on more than the present staff is competent to handle. The great growing pains suggest the need for more people and especially for managers who know the field and are well qualified to make the important decisions.

All that has been said above suggests large deficiencies in the staffing of the various departments. The salaries have been increased, but so long as there is no further increase in revenue, one wonders how the more advanced salaries are to be paid.

Now we come back to the question that has bothered us from the beginning. So long as we do not have a modern tax system the possibility of improving the quality of state government will be negligible. What is needed is a thorough revision of the entire state tax system so that the proper people can be hired and paid well enough so that they will stay with the state. So long as we follow the policy of too little and too late we are not going to get the best-qualified people.

CHAPTER VII
State Salaries

State salaries now start at $2,280 and range as high as $16,800. Most of the state employees are in the lowest salary grouping: between $2,280 and $4,080. There are some 13,065 persons in this group. In the next higher-paying category are some 8,329 persons who are able to make from $3,660 to $6,000. This is certainly an inadequate salary for those who might well make much more in private employment. The next salary range is from $5,460 to $7,860. In this category there are some 1,580 persons. In the next higher classification are found only 579 individuals who can make as much as $6,900 to $10,200. In the next classification are found 194 persons who can make from $9,180 to $12,120. In the top category there are only 100 persons who can make from $10,800 to $16,800.

Another way of stating the costs of government is to point out that New York has 230 employees per civil service worker, while New Jersey has 467 employees per civil service worker. In both cases this includes municipalities.

"It can be generally concluded that in terms of the median State job classes have kept pace with the rise in the cost of living. However, about one half of the job classes studied are below the percentage rise in the cost of living. Another half are within 14 per cent of the percentage rise in the cost of living. This 28 per cent might be considered reasonable deviation from an exact parity with cost of living rise and the result of other factors. However, classes beyond these limits are definitely below or above reasonable standards for comparison with cost of living increases. Employees of those classes below the middle fifty per cent are in jobs whose salaries have not been increased in proportion to the increased cost of living and may very well be experiencing real income hardship."[1]

"In this respect we have considered that those classes below the range of the middle fifty per cent of the increases should receive attention in order to move them up into the band (to 60%)

1. *Salary Study Program,* 1957-58, p. 2. The following quotations are from this source with the page references appearing at the end of each.

at the earliest possible opportunity. Included in this group are 11% of the $600 increment group, 23% of the $420 increment group, 15% of the $300 increment group, 11% of the $240 group, 10% of the $180 group and 8% of the $120 group and total 206 classes.'' (2)

"It is time we took a good look at our Compensation Schedule. Is it a sound framework for our Compensation Plan? Is it in tune with modern principles of salary administration? Is it working to build employee morale rather than discourage it?" (Part II, p. 1)

The private industry survey team that studied the state's personnel administration in 1954 had this to say about the schedule: "A study should be made to determine whether the distinctions between job ranges are too small for efficient administration." (1)

The progression from one range to the next higher range varies from about 6 percent to as low as 2 percent. Generally it is considered extremely difficult to justify such small distinctions between job values. We believe that a plan with fewer ranges would be easier to administer and perhaps be more acceptable from an employee standpoint.

"Private industry plans usually provide for more frequent increases during the first and sometimes the second years of employment in beginning level jobs. Since the State is competing with industry for employees, consideration should be given to modifying the State plan to provide more frequent increases in the early years of employment on beginning jobs." (1)

In a chapter on the characteristics of salary grades by Edward N. Hay, of the Pennsylvania Company, the author wrote:

"The 'rule of reason' is this: All the values in a salary scale should be geometrically related to each other--i.e., percentage-wise. This general statement may be amplified by the following detailed statements:

"A. The midpoint of each grade should be a constant percentage greater than the grade preceding it.

B. Similarly, each minimum should be approximately a constant percentage above the minimum of the grade below it, and the same applies to the maxima.

C. The 'spread' from the minimum to the maximum in grade should be a constant percentage of the minimum. That is, if the spread is to be one-third (33%)

then each maximum should be one-third (33%) greater than the minimum of the grade.

D. Salary increases should be approximately a constant percentage of the salary midpoint for each grade. Any exceptions to this rule should be made on a systematic basis. For example: the increase might be about 6% in the lower grades, tapering to 4% in the higher grades.

E. The correct number of salary grades in any situation, and therefore the percentage of 'rate of progression from grade to grade, is a matter of convenience or preference.' " (2)

"When our present schedule was designed it probably was consistent with current practice and had some relation to the conventional spread standard of 25% between minimum and maximum. However, a long series of grade adjustments have distorted this spread principle so that today we have but few ranges reflecting the 25% standard. Spreads in our schedule range from 17.2% to 27.7% with an average spread for 42 ranges of 21.1%. Fifteen ranges (35%) have spreads of less than 20%, 37 ranges (88%) have spreads of less than 25%. Only 5 ranges have spreads of 25% or more, (the two bottom ranges and three among the 600 increment group). This is of course substandard with respect to the concept stated above. This probably has a marked effect in the 120 and 180 increment brackets that is injurious to employee morale. The maximums are not high enough in relation to the minimums even though the minimums may be 'in the market' (compatible with community rates)." (3)

"Salary administration experts hold that a salary increase to be effective should be about 5%. Here, we are talking about in grade increases such as our 'increment.' In our compensation schedule, with the exception of three salary grades, our increases are less than 5%. In a few grades they are less than 3%. The smallness of the increases, especially on the lower salary levels, is too easily overlooked with the accepted use of our increment system. An increment of $120, without considering deductions, for a salary $3,960 is only 3%, likewise an increment of $180 for a salary of $5,820 is 3% and a $300 increment for a salary of $9,900 is about 2.9%. These are all at least 2% below effective standards for increments." (3)

"After usual deductions that the average employee will have, the percent and 'take home dollar' increase is even less. The illustrations show the paycheck of typical employees in the $120 bracket and in the $180 bracket, *before and after a one increment raise*. This is significant." (3)

After he gets his pay increase the employee's salary rises from $106.60 to $109.52 on the $120 increment.

"In order to correct this situation a new compensation schedule is needed, one that is based upon the concepts expressed by the American Management writers. However, the conversion to a new schedule will cost money. Also a short term morale risk is involved. This morale factor may result from the fact that to make the adjustments, employees will receive raises that are of a different amount, which to them will be different for no apparent reason." (4)

"Therefore, it is recommended that the Compensation Schedule that follows be substituted for the present compensation schedule. This schedule has been worked out to provide a *spread of 30% between minimum and maximum for each range, increments of 5% for each range that the first and second increments be awarded at six months intervals*." (4 and 5)

PROPOSED COMPENSATION SCHEDULE

30% Spread
5% Increments
5% Intervals

Range No.	Increment	Min. (Start)	2nd (6 mos.)	3rd (1 yr.)	4th (2 yrs.)	5th (3 yrs.)	6th (4 yrs.)	Max. (5 yrs.)
1	$120	$2,400	$2,520	$2,640	$2,760	$2,880	$3,000	$3,120
2	126	2,520	2,646	2,772	2,898	3,024	3,150	3,276
3	132	2,464	2,778	2,910	3.042	3,174	3,306	3,428
4	139	2,778	2,917	3,056	3,195	3,334	3,473	3,612
5	146	2,917	3,063	3,209	3,355	3,501	3,647	3,793
6	153	3,063	3,216	3,369	3,522	3,675	3,828	3,981
7	161	3,216	3,377	3,538	3,699	3,860	4,021	4,182
8	169	3,377	3,546	3,715	3,884	4,053	4,222	4,391
9	177	3,546	3,723	3,900	4,077	4,254	4,431	4,608
10	186	3,723	3,909	4,095	4,281	4,467	4,653	4,839
11	195	3,909	4,104	4,299	4,494	4,689	4,884	5,079
12	205	4,104	4,309	4,514	4,719	4,924	5,129	5,334
13	215	4,309	4,524	4,739	4,954	5,169	5,384	5,599
14	226	4,524	4,750	4,976	5,202	5,428	5,654	5,880
15	238	4,750	4,988	5,226	5,464	5,702	5,940	6,178
16	249	4,988	5,237	5,486	5,735	5,984	6,233	6,482
17	262	5,237	5,499	5,761	6,023	6,285	6,547	6,809
18	275	5,499	5,774	6,049	6,324	6,599	6,874	7,149
19	289	5,774	6,063	6,352	6,641	6,930	7,219	7,508

		(Start)	(1 yr.)	(2 yrs.)	(3 yrs.)	(4 yrs.)	(5 yrs.)	(6 yrs.)
20	303	6,063	6,366	6,669	6,972	7,275	7,578	7,881
21	318	6,366	6,684	7,002	7,320	7,638	7,956	8,274
22	334	6,684	7,018	7,352	7,686	8,020	8,354	8,688
23	351	7,018	7,369	7,720	8,071	8,422	8,773	9,124
24	368	7,369	7,737	8,105	8,473	8,841	9,209	9,577
25	387	7,737	8,124	8,511	8,898	9,285	9,672	10,059
26	406	8,124	8,530	8,936	9,342	9,748	10,154	10,560
27	427	8,530	8,957	9,384	9,811	10,238	10,665	11,092
28	448	8,957	9,405	9,853	10,301	10,749	11,197	11,645
29	470	9,405	9,875	10,345	10,815	11,285	11,755	12,225
30	494	9,875	10,369	10,863	11,357	11,851	12,345	12,839
31	518	10,369	10,887	11,405	11,923	12,441	12,959	13,477
32	544	10,887	11,431	11,975	12,519	13,063	13,607	14,151
33	572	11,431	12,003	12,575	13,147	13,719	14,291	14,863
34	600	12,003	12,603	13,203	13,803	14,403	15,003	15,603
35	630	12,603	13,233	13,863	14,493	15,123	15,753	16,383
36	662	13,233	13,895	14,557	15,219	15,881	16,543	17,205
37	695	13,895	14,590	15,285	15,980	16,675	17,370	18,065

"New Jersey Salary Ranges Compared with Those of New York, New York City, Pennsylvania, Philadelphia, Connecticut and the Federal Government

"An anslysis of current New Jersey salary ranges for a selected cross section of like jobs compared with the averages of the ranges of the jurisdiction included shows that, of the 88 jobs reported, New Jersey is lower in 60% of the cases. Fifty-five percent of our minimums are lower and 70% of our maximums are lower. In 30% of the cases our ranges are higher at both the minimum and at the maximum. However, on the average the New Jersey ranges are 5% lower than the averaged ranges of the jurisdictions studied.

"In the selected occupational and service areas listed below, New Jersey ranges are, on the average, lower by the percentage indicated:

Clericals	8.5%
Business Machine Operators	6.0%
College Level Professionals	4.4%
Trades	2.4%
Engineering	7.1%

Semiskilled and Laboring	5.9%
Nursing	4.6%
Agriculture	12.7%
Management	6.8%
Isolated Classes:	
Assistant Buyer	20.3%
Right of Way Negotiator	22.4%
Fingerprint Operator	12.5%

If differences between our rates and the average paid in the other jurisdictions range from 4.4 percent to 12.7 percent in specific occupational areas, this is evidence that selective, rather than merely general, revision is indicated for the areas identified on a relative percentage basis in order to pay rates that are in the public service market.

PRIVATE INDUSTRY SURVEY

Although our ranges have generally kept pace with increases in industry since 1955 we are still 14 percent off industry averages. (V, I)

	Industry Up Since 1955	State Up Since 1955	Industry Higher Than State (1958)
Clericals	12%	9.5%	6%
Business Machine Operators	12.5%	14%	4%
Technical and Professional	11%	21%	16.5%
Trades	14.5%	15.7%	25%
Semiskilled and Laboring	10.5%	12.3%	26%

These data suggest that if there is to be a qualified civil service, the state needs to pay considerably higher salaries to those in the employ of state and local governments. Under present circumstances little can be done, for many individuals will refuse to work for the state as long as opportunities for advancement are so limited. Certainly the government should

COMPENSATION SCHEDULE

For the New Jersey State Service Effective January 1, 1959
30% Spread
5% Increments
5% Intervals

ANNUAL SALARIES

Range No.	Incre- ment	Min. Start	2nd 1 yrs.	3rd 2 yrs.	4th 3 yrs.	5th 4 yrs.	6th 5 yrs.	Max. 6 yrs.
1	$120	$2,400	$2,520	$2,640	$2,760	$2,880	$3,000	$3,120
2	126	2,520	2,646	2,772	2,898	3,024	3,150	3,276
3	132	2,646	2,778	2,910	3,042	3,174	3,306	3,438
4	139	2,778	2,917	3,056	3,195	3,334	3,473	3,612
5	146	2,917	3,063	3,209	3,355	3,501	3,647	3,793
6	153	3,063	3,216	3,369	3,522	3,675	3,828	3,981
7	161	3,216	3,377	3,538	3,699	3,860	4,021	4,182
8	169	3,377	3,546	3,715	3,884	4,053	4,222	4,391
9	177	3,546	3,723	3,900	4,077	4,254	4,431	4,608
10	186	3,723	3,909	4,095	4,281	4,467	4,653	4,839
11	195	3,909	4,104	4,299	4,494	4,689	4,884	5,079
12	205	4,104	4,309	4,515	4,719	4,924	5,129	5,334
13	215	4,309	4,524	4,739	4,954	5,169	5,384	5,599
14	226	4,524	4,750	4,976	5,202	5,428	5,654	5,880
15	238	4,750	4,988	5,226	5,464	5,702	5,940	6,178
16	249	4,988	5,237	5,486	5,735	5,984	6,233	6,482
17	262	5,237	5,499	5,761	6,023	6,285	6,547	6,809
18	275	5,499	5,774	6,049	6,324	6,599	6,874	7,149
19	289	5,774	6,063	6,352	6,641	6,930	7,219	7,508
20	303	6,063	6,366	6,669	6,972	7,275	7,578	7,881
21	318	6,366	6,684	7,002	7,320	7,638	7,956	9,274
22	334	6,684	7,018	7,352	7,686	9,020	8,354	8,688
23	351	7,018	7,369	7,720	8,071	8,422	9,773	9,124
24	368	7,369	7,737	9,105	8,473	8,841	9,209	9,577
25	387	7,737	8,124	8,511	8,898	9,285	9,672	10,059
26	406	8,124	8,530	8,936	9,342	9,748	10,143	10,560
27	427	8,530	8,957	9,384	9,811	10,238	10,665	11,092
28	448	8,957	9,405	9,853	10,301	10,749	11,197	11,645
29	470	9,405	9,875	10,345	10,815	11,285	11,755	12,225
30	494	9,875	10,369	10,863	11,357	11,851	12,345	12,839
31	518	10,369	10,887	11,405	11,923	12,441	12,959	13,477
32	544	10,887	11,431	11,975	12,519	13,063	13,607	14,151
33	572	11,431	12,003	12,575	13,147	13,719	14,291	14,863
34	600	12,003	12,603	13,203	13,803	14,403	15,003	15,603
35	630	12,603	13,233	13,863	14,493	15,123	15,753	16,383

HOURLY RATES

						MAX.
AF	.08	1.64	1.72	1.80	1.88	1.96
AH	.09	1.73	1.82	1.91	2.00	2.09
AM	.10	2.00	2.10	2.20	2.30	2.40
AN	.11	2.10	2.21	2.32	2.43	2.54

compete with industrial rates of pay or it will get only inferior workers. Good government costs money, and unless we raise the pay level of the workers for both state and local governments the situation will not change.

New York and California pay at a much higher rate than is found in New Jersey. The federal government also pays at a higher rate than we do. This matter of pay again revives the need for a better system of taxation and for much greater revenue in New Jersey. But this cannot be accomplished so long as the property tax dominates the tax system. There should be either an income tax or a sales tax. Eventually both will be needed. These are the only taxes that will reflect the rise of costs that accompanies inflation. If the state is to stay solvent, more must be paid for a variety of services, including education, institutions and agencies, highways, water, parks, and so forth.

On January 1, 1959, the state adopted a new salary schedule, This provides for the following pay scales: refer to table on page 68.

Two facts are of interest here. First, the provision for a sixth months' increase was eliminated. Second, the provision that someone might be paid between $13,233 and $17,205 has been eliminated.

There is doubt that the state can afford to pay such salaries so long as the present tax system remains in effect. Large additions to the civil service personnel will create a serious problem. In the current budget some $5 million has been set aside for the purpose of increasing salaries. But if recovery does not develop soon, several people will be wondering where their money is coming from.

CHAPTER VIII

Critical Evaluation of New Jersey's Tax System

The critical problem of New Jersey is the lack of adequate financial powers to pay for the needed improvements in the quality of the various state services. This has been shown by the earlier summary of the needs of the state and the deficiencies in the quality of governmental services. Few areas have not accumulated deficiencies of substantial proportions. Perhaps the greatest lack is found in the field of education: the State University has been neglected and the public schools have been dependent upon the property tax as their primary means of support.

The reason for this failure is easy to find. It is the tradition of "no new taxes" and the resistance to reform of the tax system. Even in the 1957 campaign each candidate made it clear that there would be no new taxes if he was elected. In spite of this implied promise, the new 1 3/4 per cent corporation tax has been added to the roster of state taxes and there is a rather well-organized campaign to impose a sales tax upon the citizens of the state. The mention of an income tax frightens almost everyone, but only an income tax could raise money in a more equitable fashion than a sales tax. Eventually the state may well have to impose both taxes. The costs of government will continue to rise as the need for schools, colleges and the university, roads, highways, institutions and agencies, and parks grows apace. The great difficulty is that the state has neglected its obligations for such a long period of time that everything will cost more in the future than it would now.

New six-lane highways will be much more costly than the old two-lane highways; the divider and the need to condemn existing improvements will add to the cost. New educational facilities are going to become more expensive as they involve the acquisition of improved land. Teachers will cost more. Governmental cost also will rise as the salary schedules of the state are not yet high enough to get the sort of individuals needed to run the government. The longer the state postpones the acquisition of land for parks the more expensive the job will become. Institutions and agencies will have to raise their salary schedules if they are to find personnel capable of giving the sick and mentally deficient the care demanded by modern medicine.

For the past fifty years or more New Jersey has lagged in bringing its tax system into line with more modern thinking and has endeavored to get by without the use of a broad-based tax. The new corporation tax is a tax upon the wealth of the corporation but can hardly be considered a tax with a broad base. The chief characteristic of the state has been its dependence upon the property tax and its refusal to think about the other taxes that have been real revenue producers in other states. The result has been to create wide differentials in the capacities of various communities to finance schools, parks, and roads and has left the state with inadequate funds to provide properly for other government costs.

In addition, the taxes imposed upon the railroads, the inventory tax, and the tax on improvements have left the state in an unfavorable position when appealing to firms with heavy inventories or heavy investments in plant and equipment.

The story of the railroad tax is of considerable interest. This was long one of the favorite taxes used in Hudson County, where the bulk of the yards are located, and the political machine in that county was successful in keeping the matter of the railroad tax out of consideration at the time of the constitutional convention. The sensitivity of the Hudson County bosses made it expedient to concede this defeat as one of the ways of gaining agreement on other much-needed constitutional revision. Yet it was the Hudson County delegation that imposed the wording that has since caused them so much trouble: the statement that the property of the state should be valued at a reasonable rate including that of the railroads. The interesting question remains—determining the proper valuation of the railroad yards located in Hudson County.

When the previous chapter has been assessed it will indicate how backward the state has been in the revision of its tax system.

The following quotations from the various reports of the Commission on State Tax Policy are as severe an indictment of the state tax system as could be imagined:

State of New Jersey. *First Report of the Commission on State Tax Policy* Appointed Pursuant to Laws of 1945, ch. 157 (approved April 12, 1945).

Submitted to the Governor and to the Legislature, April 28, 1946.

Trenton, New Jersey.

Members of the Commission:

> John F. Sly, Chairman
> W. Paul Stillman, Vice Chairman
> Amos Dixon
> Charles English
> Jacob S. Glickenhaus
> Norman F. S. Russell
> David Van Alstyne, Jr.

Pages viii and ix (footnote 5):

"Recent studies on comparative tax costs have developed another factor which, while still helping to make New Jersey 'a favorable tax State from the standpoint of operating business,' is not as comforting as those factors mentioned above. The application of New Jersey property tax rates to the full value of all taxable real estate and personal property owned by business firms would in most instances produce an excessive tax. The average property tax rate in the State was $4.74 (1944) for each $100 of valuation taxable. This means a potential tax liability amounting to 4.74 per cent of the value of real and tangible personal property *each year*; and many of new Jersey's most highly industrialized areas have property tax rates in excess of the average State rate. . . .

"Property taxes account, moreover, for most of the taxes paid by business in New Jersey. While corporate business now pays a tax upon net worth, this tax is neither large nor burdensome. Six New Jersey corporations reporting to the Commission on Taxation of Intangible Personal Property showed that their total taxes in New Jersey for 1944 (exclusive of unemployment compensation taxes), amounted to substantially less than their income in excise taxes alone would have amounted to had these businesses been located in New York or Massachusetts *(Report,* March 26, 1945, p. 39). While these comparisons were made before the recent change in corporation taxes *(Laws of 1945, ch. 162),* they would require little modification today.

"A recent study of comparative tax costs (New York City, Department of Commerce, *Report on the Relative Costs within*

*Seven Selected Cities for Three Groups of Manufacturing
Industries,* (New York, September, 1944), indicated that Newark
ranks second in terms of State and local taxes (1944) among the
seven cities considered. It is, however, significant, that both
the highest and lowest tax paid by individual corporations included in the study, were found in Newark. In actual practice,
the New Jersey property tax provisions are rarely applied in
full measure. For this reason, any tax comparisons between
New Jersey locations and locations in other states can be based
only upon actual tax practices as they are applied to actual
business firms. In instances where this has been done, New
Jersey has usually been found to be a 'favorable tax State.' "

Page xviii:

". . .The Commission would repeat that no other great industrial State has done so little in the past fifty years to bring
its tax structure into line with its social, economic and political development. It is not possible to overcome this long
neglect with a single statute or a series of statutes. So deep
have been the effects of an archaic tax structure that the dis-
turbance of a single exemption or even the adjustment of an
important tax payer threatens to disrupt significant parts of the
economy."

State of New Jersey. *Second Report of the Commission on State
          Tax Policy.*
          Submitted to the Governor and to the Legislature,
          March 24, 1947
          Trenton, New Jersey.
          Members of the Commission:
                    John F. Sly, Chairman
                    W. Paul Stillman, Vice Chairman
                    Amos F. Dixon
                    Charles R. English
                    Jacob S. Glickenhaus
                    Norman F. S. Russell
                    Charles K. Barton

Letter of transmittal, page ix:

"The Commission believes that the present situation with
respect to the tangible personal property tax is intolerable. It

also believes that some new manner of taxing this type of property must be adopted, and that the longer the present situation is permitted to continue the more difficult the readjustment will become.''

Page xi:

"This Commission's Report, submitted herewith, represents a sincere effort to repair a major part of our present tax system within the very restricted frame of reference permitted by the shibboleths which have impaired every effort to achieve an equitable tax system in New Jersey. The Commission deems it essential that the people of New Jersey realize that the proposals of this Report represent perhaps the last of the revenue possibilities to be realized through the process of tax adjustment and replacement. It is not the province of the Commission to pass upon any or all of the rising demands for new and improved services by our State and local governments. But when these demands are made, it should be clearly understood that there is little remaining of possible sources of State or local revenue within our present tax structure which can support any substantial expenditure program. It is perfectly true that we have not to this point added any new and additional taxes, but this can be no more than a soporific observation. A careful examination of the constantly rising municipal tax rates is sufficient to prove that we are raising and expending new and additional tax dollars every year—and we are raising those tax dollars through an indifferently administered and inequitable tax system. Even if it were perfectly administered, our tax system would still fall far short of the requirements of a modern industrial State.

"The difference between the potential tax of $100,000,000 which legally could have been assessed to business under the present law and the actual tax of $28,000,000 represents the major potential 'tax lightning' inherent in our present system. That is, as municipalities feel the pressure for added tax revenues, they may turn, and in some cases have turned to sharp increases in assessments on business tangibles, assessments which were either sudden reversals of former policy or arbitrary impositions on selected taxpayers. So long as these assessments do not exceed true value the taxpayer has no effective remedy, and may even be subject to the 'omitted property' provisions of the law which permit the added assessments

to be made retroactive for two years. This is what is meant by
'tax lightning.'

"This is not to imply that any such complete exploitation of
personal property is either contemplated or economically fea-
sible. It has long been recognized, either as a matter of law in
states which have met the problem through a variety of statu-
tory devices, or as a matter of practice in such States as New
Jersey, that personal property, particularly inventories of stock
in trade, semi-finished goods, work in process and raw materials, is totally unsuited to taxation ad valorem under the general
property tax. *In this sense, personal property is not now and
never has been truly a part of the general property tax base.*
But the letter of the law which places it within that base has
caused negotiation to be substituted for taxation, and an un-
healthy atmosphere of caprice to take the place of clear-cut
official responsibility. The result, to be expected under such
conditions, has been discriminatory, unequal and sometimes
arbitrary assessments."

Page xiv:

"The Commission recommends that machinery, tools, equipment, furniture and fixtures used in business be state-assessed
at true value, which shall be presumed to be book value but not
less than twenty per cent of cost so long as an item remains in
use; and that such property be assessed at one-half of the local
general property tax rate, but not in excess of the previous
year's average state rate. This will yield $16 million annually,
in place of the present $11.6 million, to be returned to the re-
spective municipalities in which the property is located.

"It is perfectly clear that the treatment of tangible business
personalty, particularly business inventories, under the general
property tax, however assessed, is entirely undesirable from an
economic viewpoint. The economic objection is directed prin-
cipally toward any effort to assess inventories of finished
goods, work in process or raw materials on an ad valorem
basis. This type of property, which has borne the brunt of the
present personal property tax on business ($17 million out of a
total of $28.6 million in 1946) has greatly varying characteris-
tics from industry to industry, so that in some industries inventory may turn over twice a year whereas in others it may
turn over twelve times a year or more. The value of raw
materials and work in process is especially questionable in
those industries where spoilage is an important factor. While

slow-moving inventory may be kept on the books at the same value as rapidly moving inventory, it obviously has vastly different characteristics as a tax source. It is well known, moreover, that inventory is readily controllable in some industries, and any attempt to effective application of an ad valorem tax would merely result in a flight of such inventories out of the State. In brief, inventory is mobile, is consumption goods, whereas other forms of personal property are relatively fixed in location and are production goods. It is neither logical nor practical to tax them the same way."

Page xvi:

"The Commission recommends that the present property tax as applied to business inventories of raw materials, work in process, semi-finished goods and stock in trade be abolished, and that in lieu thereof there be adopted a 'general business excise tax' at the rate of 2/10 of 1 per cent upon the value of goods produced in New Jersey, in the case of manufacturers, and on the gross volume of business in this State, in the case of all other enterprise (with certain exceptions). This will yield $24.0 million annually in place of the present $17.0 million raised from business inventories."

Page xviii:

"The Commission recommends that the taxation of household goods as property be completely abandoned, and that the municipalities be given the power to impose as a matter of local home rule an occupancy tax which would apply in such manner as the local governing body may determine. It is further recommended that the taxation of farm personalty remain as at present to be administered under the general property tax."

Page 2:

"We have succeeded in maintaining our tax position only because we were able to use some $109,000,000 of highway revenues for non-highway purposes during the depression years, and only because we have engaged in a continual process of patching and repairing our failing tax system. By any measure of a fair distribution of the cost of government, we have suffered and still suffer under the grossest inequities and inequalities."

Page 36:

"More recently, the Committee on Taxation of the Twentieth Century Fund under the chairmanship of Thomas I. Parkinson, aided by Professors Carl Shoup, Roy Blough, and Mabel Newcomer, reported on a survey of taxation in the United States and concluded: 'In common with practically every other observer, past or present, we deplore the obvious injustices found under the property tax. We urge that they be speedily lessened, even though complete elimination is too much to hope for. Continual pressure for better assessors and better assessment under the real estate tax must be exerted. Whether state assessment rather than local assessment is called for is a matter that must be decided in each state in the light of local conditions, but we should like to see a few states, at least, try the experiment. *There are substantial reasons for abolishing the tax on tangible personal property in any state that can possibly raise its revenue in another way. It is difficult to administer. Even if it is perfectly administered, it is a poor means of measuring either the benefit to or the ability of an individual or a business firm.'* "

Page 66:

"While the household goods item appears substantial, it is subject to an extraordinary degree of delinquency, the amount of which cannot be estimated accurately. In some communities, the amount of household assessments is collected as fully as the real estate assessments, but in the larger cities it has been found entirely impractical to administer the present tax on household goods. For example, the city of Newark reports that on the basis of past experience, its results for 1946 will be:

Household Personalty Tax Assessed	$ 333,716.76
Amount Uncollectible	$ 223,078.32
Amount cancelled according to law	$ 21,533.16
Amount Paid or to be Paid for the Current Year	$ 89,105.28
Percentage Uncollectible	73.3%"

The failure of the state to recognize the need for some broad-based tax has been its most serious fault. Without money it is impossible to carry out an adequate state financial program. Without funds little can be done to raise the state to the level of other states of comparable wealth. Perhaps the greatest need is for more state aid for education generally and for the development of a really first-class university. The State Colleges also need to receive more assistance if they are to develop into first-class liberal arts institutions.

But so long as the state has an inadequate income to finance those services only one choice remains: an individual income tax or a sales tax. The use by Indiana of a gross receipts tax is not recommended, as it fails to make any differentiation between the high markup and the low markup stores as well as to recognize the fact of varying rates of turnover among different classes of business. What can be said about the gross receipts tax is that it has the advantage of a deceptively low rate but is one of the more inequitable taxes that can be imposed by any state government. One other possibility remains, the use of a value added tax such as that recently repealed in Michigan. This would have some advantages for New Jersey, as it is also a state that exports a large percentage of manufactured goods. This would be one way of gaining at the expense of those who buy these exported products. Yet the fear of competition and the desire to avoid any deterrent to the growth of new business in the state would probably make this a less attractive tax than either the sales or the individual income tax. We must also remember that the existing tax structure is about as regressive as any tax structure can be and would be made even more regressive by the use of a value added tax.

The Individual Income Tax

The severity of federal rates has left the states in a difficult position so far as the further use of the individual income tax is concerned. Though this tax is ideal from the point of view of equity, the resistance of the states to the use of the individual income tax has resulted in no state's adopting this tax since 1937. Although the District of Columbia has added a tax since that time, the lack of representation permitted this to be done.

New Jersey has the necessary wealth to raise a lot of money from an individual income tax. How many individuals would leave the state as the result of the imposition of such a tax is difficult to estimate, but the wealth that remains in New York and in Westchester County suggests that the movement would be smaller than many imagine. It is also true that a great many individuals find it convenient to live in New Jersey as a means of quick access to their jobs in lower Manhattan.

The advantages of the individual income tax are many. First, it permits the exemption of a minimum below which no tax is levied. So long as the state imposes as great a burden as it now does on property this exemption would tend to equalize the distribution of the tax burden among income classes. We must also remember that the cigarette tax, the gasoline tax, and a considerable part of the tax burden imposed upon business are probably passed along to the consumer.

A further great advantage of the individual income tax is the possibility of the use of progressive rate schedules. Although no state goes nearly so far as the federal government in the use of progression, the possibility of such a tax would do much to restore the equity that is needed in New Jersey's tax system. One should also remember that the federal government permits the deduction of state tax in the computation of federal income tax. This means that a large part of the federal tax liability is being diverted to the use of the state that uses an income tax. When the effective rate is as much as 7 per cent, the federal government contributes much of the tax due the state.

Still another advantage of the use of an income tax by the state to raise revenue is that New York has agreed to permit each individual to deduct from his New York State tax liability the full amount paid to the state of residence. In other words, all the commuters living in Northern New Jersey would pay little more to both New York and New Jersey, unless they had sizable investment income which New York cannot claim within its income tax. The possibility that New York would give up this credit for tax paid in state of residence is remote, since Connecticut and Pennsylvania are involved, as well as New Jersey, and the danger of driving many firms out of New York would be substantial.

For those with substantial investment income the imposition of a New Jersey income tax would prove a substantial burden. But if the state needs the money, who is better able to pay than this group? A final feature of the individual income tax is the ability to adjust it to the needs of individuals. The federal government has gone further than I would like to see it go in this regard, but the possibility of deduction for medical expenses, the taxation of capital gains, the possibility of special deductions for the disabled, and so forth make the individual income tax one of the most sensitive taxes that can be imagined. The danger is that the interest groups will take advantage of the law and develop some deductions that are not deserved. The deferred compensation schemes are now given to almost all executives in industry. No tax is free from some abuses but if there is to be a tax the advantages of the individual income tax are substantial.

The revenue potential of a tax imposed at New York State rates would be approximately $135 million to $140 million per year if there was no depression. It would also grow as the state grew and income rose. If we set our tax system in order, the possibilities of the use of an income tax would be greatly improved. The danger is that the people would resist the imposition of an income tax, as the severity of the federal rates has made them too conscious of the demands of the central government. In a poll taken recently in California, where most of the people pay a 4 per cent sales tax—3 per cent to the state and 1 per cent to the county—the sales tax was more popular than the individual income tax. This in spite of the fact that they have $3,500 exemptions for a married couple and that the brackets are $5,000 wide, so that a man with two children will not pay more than 1 per cent of his taxable income until his income is over $14,000. This is due to the community property law which has been in effect in California for many years. This finding suggests that the first tax that will be imposed in New Jersey is much more liable to be a sales tax than an income tax. If state services could be supported more fully by the imposition of a sales tax, there would be substantial advantages to the use of this levy, since the primary difficulty at the present time is a deficiency in level of state services.

Sales Tax

This suggestion that a sales tax is the most likely one to be used by New Jersey is based upon the reaction of the public to the severity of the federal income tax and the well organized resistance to the use of an income tax in the state. The public information necessary to gain acceptance for an income tax has been lacking and the sales tax has some strong advocates. Even labor cannot persuade its own people that the income tax has considerable advantages over the sales tax.

The sales tax has some real advantages over the current system of selective excises. In the first place, it does not discriminate among persons according to their habits. In the second place, it is a less regressive tax than the property tax or most of the taxes imposed upon the selective sales items. Its greatest disadvantage is the difficulty of collection. So long as the rest of New York State does not impose a sales tax there is always the possibility that some individuals will make their major purchases in New York City and have the goods shipped to New Jersey. In the case of automobiles registration makes it easy to enforce the law. In the case of durable goods the law would be much more difficult to enforce, and many individuals might make their major purchases in the region adjacent to Northern New Jersey and bring goods back in their automobiles. A use tax can be imposed but it would be difficult to enforce. The existence of a sales tax in Pennsylvania is of substantial benefit, and a New Jersey tax would reduce the number of trips to Philadelphia. If and when New York State imposes a sales tax, the problem of enforcement will become a lot easier.

The yield of a sales tax at a 3 per cent rate would be approximately $212 million if everything was included. The yield of a 4 per cent tax, with food exempt, would be approximately $206 million. The real question is: should food be exempted or left within the base? This is a serious matter, for the lower the family's income the higher the percentage of the total budget that must be spent for food. One must also remember that housing cannot be inlcuded within the sales tax base because of the high percentage of owner-occupied homes. There is also the question of inclusion and exclusion of such items as medicine, the value of plant and equipment expenditures, and so forth. Including the valuation of plant and equipment will cause the yield of the sales tax to be much more variable than if it was left out. Other questions arise about the inclusion of children's clothing, the cost of meals purchased away from home, and doctor's bills. It is my belief that the exemption of food would be a wise move, although restaurant meals could be taxed. Yet there is little question about the resistance of the public to the inclusion of the above-mentioned items. This suggests the strong possibility that the exemption of food, medicine, doctors' bills, and even clothing will be considered. If this is done, the problems of enforcement are going to be much greater than they should be and the danger of evasion will be increased.

The advantages of a sales tax are not to be overlooked. Everyone pays something. But unfortunately it is unlikely that any substantial portion of the new revenue produced by a sales tax can be used to relieve the burden upon real estate. This is due to the rapid growth in the population and the need for still better schools and colleges. When the additional costs of highways, parks, and institutions and agencies are added, as well as the improved salary schedules needed at the state and local level, there is little chance that the property owner will get much relief as the result of the imposition of a sales tax. What can be hoped for is that property tax rates will not be forced up as much as they otherwise would and that the quality of the performance of the state and local governments can be vastly improved. There is still another need—the need for water. The cost of water will become one of the more important items over the next few years, and if a real job of planning for the state is done little or nothing will be left for the real estate owner or renter. What can be hoped for is that the poorer sections of the state will have a much higher level of education and parks and better teachers as the result of a substantial increase in the amount of state aid.

A sales tax has another advantage. It is much less regressive and would be preferable to a further increase in the most regressive of all taxes—the real estate tax—or in the further exploitation of some of the selective sales taxes. And with food and housing exempt, the sales tax would produce a roughly proportionate amount for a considerable period.

The real danger is that organized labor will fight a sales tax in so far as it is able, and may make the use of this instrument a difficult choice for the legislature. If the leaders could persuade their members to favor an income tax, this position would make some sense, but at present the need for more revenue becomes the dominant consideration. Certainly the ability of the state to continue on its present precarious financial course is well-nigh exhausted, and the people will suffer so long as this is the case. Inadequate service levels have never made a state prosperous, and in view of what is clearly to be foreseen the need for much greater revenue is clear and unmistakable.

There is still another danger. The Governor may well consider it his obligation to veto any bill that proposes a sales tax. In view of his campaign promises this would be a moral obligation, and as recently as the spring of 1959 he stated that he would not favor either an income tax or a sales tax. Perhaps he will now see the light, in view of the serious financial plight of the state.

The greatest danger of all is that nothing will be done for some time. If so, the result will be a general deterioration in the quality of government at the cost of the youth of the state, the problems of traffic, the quality of the institutions and agencies, an adequate water supply, and recreational facilities. And if salaries are raised as they should be there will be further expense and a need for still more revenue.

The wealth to finance adequate state services is now available. There must be a thorough revision of the tax system, so that the wealth of the state can be taxed. The two best methods of doing this are the individual income tax and the sales tax. In view of the severity of the federal income tax, there is little likelihood that this will be the first tax used—yet it is the more logical of the two.

The primary difficulty of the New Jersey tax system is its lack of elasticity. States with activity-based taxes (income, sales, or gross receipts) find that their revenues grow with the level of economic activity. If inflation expands the need for a given volume of public services, these same inflationary sources expand the tax base and produce the necessary additional revenues. Real economic growth is automatically reflected in higher incomes and sales receipts and these again lead to larger revenues at the same tax rates.[1]

A tax structure dominated by rigid revenue sources cannot cope with the higher outlays necessitated by inflation or by additional services. (261) The property tax has proved to be one of the least expansible of all taxes. The sales taxes that are found in New Jersey do not have the elasticity needed for new expenditures or for inflation. To finance increased expenditures, the taxing authority must raise rates—a step which puts the taxing jurisdiction in an unfavorable light compared with that of rival states seeking to attract new industry by keeping tax rates stable.

A state that lacks elastic revenue sources is particularly vulnerable to inflation. Its expenditures rise with the general rise in prices, but the tax sources do not produce proportionately higher receipts unless rates are increased or the base is expanded. And if, during the period of inflation, it becomes necessary to provide a larger quantity or a higher quality of governmental services, the problem of financing is further compounded. These considerations cast doubt on the wisdom of self-imposed tax restrictions and indicate the need for a thorough re-examination of New Jersey's fiscal structure. (261)

1. *Government Finance in New Jersey,* by Morris Beck. Flink, *op. cit.,* pp. 560-561. The following quotations are from this source with the page reference appearing at the end of each.

The tradition against new taxes has not prevented the property tax from rising as the needs related to the growth of population, the movement to suburbia, new roads, and the technological revolution of our times call for increased services from the state. Since 1951 the property tax base (at full value) has increased from $15,616,974,000 to $25,052,285,153. This increase has left the property owner in the unenviable position of bearing the brunt of the increased costs of government. The failure of so many school budgets suggests that the property taxpayer has decided that he will pay little more and that the maximum rate has been applied to the property tax except in a few wealthy communities. It is necessary to add that these figures represent equalized values as of October 1, 1957.

Owing to the growth of population, the rise in the use of automobiles, the movement to suburbia, and the need for new schools, firehouses, water, police, roads, and so forth, the costs of state and local governments have shown a marked rise. The actual increase has been from the per capita level of $33.10 in 1946 to $96.21 in 1956. In real terms, after adjustment for price increases, the rise turns out to be 74 per cent for New Jersey. Real expenditures also rose for the entire United States by 74 per cent in this same period.

It is of interest to note that the growth in state and local expenditures was strong enough to withstand the postwar recessions of 1948-49 and 1953-54. Quarterly data indicate that state and local expenditures continued their upward climb in each quarter of these cyclical declines. The long-run tendencies that have increased state and local spending in the past decade may be expected to remain strong in the years ahead.

The table on the following page indicating the distribution of total expenditures suggests that New Jersey is not keeping up with the neighboring states.

Maryland has been included in the Middle Atlantic states, since it has more nearly the characteristics of the industrialized states of the North than those of the southern complex. The figures reveal that New Jersey has fallen behind in its support of education, in the public welfare field, and particularly in the field of health and hospitals. The state is ahead in the field of public safety and about even in the field of general control. The danger is not that some communities do not give good education, but that the standards throughout the state depend upon the size of the tax base and the willingness of individuals to bear the greater part of the cost of education. Particularly disgraceful is the

TABLE VIII

FUNCTIONAL DISTRIBUTION OF GENERAL EXPENDITURES,
1957 (PER CAPITA)

	New Jersey	New York	Penn-sylvania	Middle Atlantic States	All States
Education	$21.77	$35.68	$39.08	$42.31	$39.37
Highways	24.94	22.21	27.60	35.66	35.79
Public Welfare	6.93	13.46	11.13	10.70	16.64
Health & Hospitals	8.47	19.54	13.04	14.79	8.5
Public Safety	4.25	3.88	3.10	2.8	2.8
Natural Resources	2.28	7.09	2.24	4.35	4.79
General Control	3.11	4.62	2.86	3.51	3.23
Miscel-laneous	$51,519,000	$208,694,000	$73,456,000	$77,854,000	$34,544,000

Source: *State Government Finances in 1957*. Bureau of the Census,
U.S. Department of Commerce, 1958. Tables 38 and 9.

deficiency in the field of public welfare and in that of health and
hospitals. The state has the capacity to support adequate facilities but the tax system does not permit the maintenance of a
real program of care and rehabilitation. The failure to spend
more for natural resources relates to the industrial characteristics of the state and the lack of many good mineral deposits in
the state.

It is of interest to note that New York spends much more on
natural resource development, but there are somewhat more
resources in that state. One should also note that expenditures
for highways are within reason and that in the past the construction of toll highways made the expenditures of the state loom
very large in relation to total expenditures. In the case of highways the need for more expenditure will again arise, and with
the new federal money now available the sums will probably be
greater in the near future. In this connection it is of interest to
remember that the density of traffic in New Jersey greatly ex-
ceeds that of either New York or Pennsylvania.

The following quotation from Beck is important as it raises

most of the questions that must be raised about the character of the New Jersey tax system:

"A. Will the present state and local tax structure at the present rates be adequate to meet the probable future expenditure pattern? If additional revenues are required, can they be obtained by merely increasing the rates of the existing taxes as has been done in the past?

"B. Can existing rates be increased without violence to accepted taxing principles of equity and fairness? Has the tax load reached the point at which a further rise in rates will involve unreasonable economic burdens for the taxpayers? In short, has the present tax system, dominated as it is by the property tax and selective excises, the elasticity to grow with the economy?

"C. For instance, will the current tax structure permit or discourage the State government to relieve municipalities of certain phases of the water resources development program? Does it have the adaptability to compensate for industrial relocations from one municipality to another; or will it adversely affect the town with the lost industry while bringing a windfall to its neighbor?" (577)

The chief reliance of the localities is upon the property tax. More than 80 per cent of municipal budgets are financed by the tax on property and more than 60 per cent of the total amount raised in the state is produced by property tax. Dependence upon this source is questioned because, although clothed with the respectability of age and the prestige of colonial origins, it must be questioned on the following grounds:

"1. The tax, broad-based in an agricultural society today reaches only a small category of income-producing assets.

"2. It is relatively insensitive to economic fluctuations because the rise and fall of property assessments does not closely follow changes in business conditions.

"3. It bears little relation to either ability to pay or benefits received from government, particularly in the case of residential properties.

"4. It accelerates economic decline by depressing property values and discouraging property rehabilitation.

"5. It is difficult to administer uniformly and equitably because there is no precise method of arriving at property values.

"6. The tax on personal property is impossible to enforce adequately because of the lack of standards of value and the immense burden of seeking out all personal property for assessment." (578)

So long as we continue to have local governments we should not consider the elimination of the property tax. But the need is for more state assistance in the financing of local services and a reduction in the burden of the property tax, or at least no further increases. The need for more state aid is clear if New Jersey is to assure its continued growth.

PROBLEMS AND PROSPECTS

The need for increased revenue will grow as the need for a higher quality of services is demanded and as the population of the state continues to grow. There is little hope that the existing revenue system can produce the needed receipts to finance both better services and proper care of an expanding population. The prospect that we must face is the adoption of both an income tax and a sales tax. The sales tax will probably come first, but the need for some base that relates to the growth of the state is essential; and either sales or income tax will reflect the increased volume of business done in the state and also further inflation if that is to be faced by the state in its purchase of goods and services. The real estate tax cannot be increased much more except in those few wealthy communities that now have the benefit of low rates.

There should be more state assistance to the local communities if education is to be made equal throughout the state and the services are to be made anything like what should be possible in a state of the wealth of New Jersey. There is no reason for the low salaries paid state officials. There is no reason for the inadequate level of our hospitals and mental institutions. There is no reason for the crowded conditions on our highways. There is no reason for the lack of adequate park space and the lack of recreational opportunity. There is no reason for the inadequate attention paid to those who are finding it difficult to make ends meet and need relief or other assistance. There is no reason for the inadequate job done in promotion of the state and the appeal to new industry. A major gain could be registered if a better job were done in the last-named area.

But in the end we come back to the basic facts of life: New Jersey's tax system makes the state unattractive to many prospective industries and the individual finds the real estate excessive. Particularly retired persons who continue to live in New Jersey find the burden of the real estate tax difficult to meet. They would be well advised to move to some other state where the tax burden is more equitably distributed.

One suggestion for solving the state's financial problems is the use of more authorities. However authorities are no substitute for more orderly governmental procedures. They are no substitute for a more adequate revenue system. They also have the disadvantage of creating independent units that are not subject to the full review of the legislature and are possibilities for graft and influence peddling. The authority is a device that permits the decisions of government to be made by individuals without appeal to the electorate. In the end there is also no assurance that the authority securities sanctioned by the state will not have to be supported by the state, whether backed by the full faith and credit of the state or not. In other words, the use of authorities is a poor way of solving the problems that confront a state as wealthy as New Jersey. If the quality of state services is raised as it should be, the requirements for state revenue may well be increased to close to $1 billion by 1975. This is assuming that there are no more price increases; in other words, in terms of 1956 prices. The current deficits in the basic state services suggest that if orderly government is to be assured, there will be a real rise in the costs of government. A foundation program of at least $400 is needed if the schools are to prosper. More college and university facilities are needed, but the money necessary to finance such an expansion is not available. The need for parks and for better mental and other hospital facilities is well known but the revenue system will not support the necessary costs. Better development of the state's resources is required if the growth of New Jersey is to be continuous. Higher salaries must be paid if the most capable people are to run the affairs of the state. Better over-all planning is essential.

The assumption underlying these estimates is that the state will spend approximately 4 per cent of its income for the services of government. This is well below the average of all the states, which spend about 6 per cent of their total income for governmental services. According to the estimates that have been worked out in the Rutgers Study, 4 per cent would give us an annual expenditure of $940 million. It would not be difficult to see this expand to a grand total of $1 billion by 1975.

Failure to maintain a good level of government services will not attract industry. Those concerned about industrial development must realize that the quality of both state and local services is just as important as the level of taxation. We get what we pay for. There is little reason to believe that low taxes and poor services will make the state an attractive one in which to locate. The major studies of taxation as it affects industrial location are negative in their findings. There are always two sides to the tax program of a state: first, level of services; second, the level of taxation.

There is little question about the need for tax reform in New Jersey. But little can be done unless and until the leadership is forthcoming. If we fail to make the state tax system responsive to changing conditions and to the extent and degree of possible inflation, then the state services will continue to deteriorate at the cost of quality and at the cost of further economic development.

The Property Tax

The property tax is one of the most regressive taxes that can be imposed upon the people of the state. The following figures taken from the Bureau of Labor Statistics survey of consumer finances in 1950 reveal the regressive nature of the property tax:

TABLE IX

1950 Per Cent of Income Spent for Rented Housing
by Those Reporting Expenditure

Northern New Jersey Area	Philadelphia, Pa., & Camden, N. J., Area
Income after Taxes	Income after Taxes
UNDER $1,000	43.31	48.78
$1,000-$2,000	24.87	22.72
$2,000-$3,000	15.87	15.75
$3,000-$4,000	13.57	12.05
$4,000-$5,000	12.03	10.54
$5,000-$6,000	9.77	9.88
$6,000-$7,500	10.11	12.36
$7,500-$10,000	6.49	9.88
OVER $10,000	9.22	6.76

Source: United States Bureau of Labor Statistics. *Study of Consumer Expenditure, Income and Savings* (Philadelphia: University of Pennsylvania, 1956), V, IV, p. 12.

1950 Owned Housing

| Northern New Jersey Area | | Philadelphia, Pa., & Camden, N. J., Area |
Income after Taxes (Per cent)		Income after Taxes (Per cent)
UNDER $1,000	----	42.23
$1,000-$2,000	30.81	16.03
$2,000-$3,000	12.33	11.27
$3,000-$4,000	12.18	10.41
$4,000-$5,000	9.86	9.74
$5,000-$6,000	10.87	7.75
$6,000-$7,500	8.51	7.43
$7,500-$10,000	8.51	10.91
OVER $10,000	6.55	7.76

United States Bureau of Labor Statistics. *Study of Consumer Expenditure, Income and Savings,* v. IV. (University of Pennsylvania, 1956), p. 12.

| Family Expenditure for Automobile Operation -1950 | | Family Expenditure for Automobile Operation by Those Reporting Expenditure |
| Northern New Jersey Area | | Philadelphia, Pa., & Camden, N. J., Area |
Income after Taxes (Per cent)		Income after Taxes (Per cent)
UNDER $1,000	10.43	----
$1,000-$2,000	14.54	----
$2,000-$3,000	10.45	10.94
$3,000-$4,000	6.28	7.20
$4,000-$5,000	6.10	6.49
$5,000-$6,000	5.23	6.05
$6,000-$7,500	3.89	5.56
$7,500-$10,000	4.13	6.85
OVER $10,000	2.39	2.47

Source: United States Bureau of Labor Statistics. *Study of Consumer Expenditure, Income and Savings,* v. iii. (University of Pennsylvania, 1956), p. 12.

	Per cent of Income Spent for Tobacco Products by Those Reporting Expenditures	Per Cent of Income Spent for Tobacco Products by Those Reporting Expenditures
	Northern New Jersey Area	Philadelphia, Pa., & Camden, N. J., Area
	Income after Taxes (Per cent)	Income after Taxes (Per cent)
UNDER $1,000	9.66	5.81
$1,000-$2,000		
$2,000-$3,000	3.73	3.72
$3,000-$4,000	2.35	3.59
$4,000-$5,000	2.84	2.99
$5,000-$6,000	2.46	2.67
$6,000-$7,500	2.12	2.49
$7,500-$10,000	1.52	2.01
OVER $10,000	.98	.94

Source: United States Bureau of Labor Statistics. *Study of Consumer Expenditure, Income and Savings,* v. III. (University of Pennsylvania, 1956). p.12

The above data reveal that New Jersey has a very regressive tax system. Even many business taxes are passed along to consumers. And so long as the line is held by the press and the politicians, who argue against new taxes, there will be little improvement in the situation. The most important tax is the property tax and this places an unduly heavy burden upon the low-income recipient. As has been stated, insult is added to injury when declining properties are more heavily taxed than better neighborhoods and the assessment ratios on higher-priced homes are less than those on the lower-class neighborhoods. Business property pays heavily for the benefits it receives, and in Hudson County it pays about twice as much as residential property. It is difficult to understand why anyone would locate in Hudson County. (See the Sixth Report of the Commission on State Tax Policy.)

Serious thought should be given to the taxpayer's problems. Few states have as poorly distributed a tax system as New Jersey. For a considerable period of time there will naturally be opposition to any increase in state taxes, but if New Jersey is to prosper there must be more state services, a higher quality of civil service, a better system of parks, more water, and a much better system of highways, better provision for education; institutions and agencies also need more money, as do most of the other state bodies.

CHAPTER IX

Conclusions

A recent piece in the *New York Times* suggests that New Jersey is worried by the failure of national economic recovery to reduce the volume of unemployment. This concern is predicated on the failure of unemployment to decline substantially over the past three months and on the aggressive competition New Jersey is facing from other states for new industrial construction.

Some business executives also insist that the uncertain tax situation in this state has recently resulted in a marked reduction in investment of out-of-state capital. A new $1\frac{3}{4}$ per cent state corporate net income tax became effective July 1, 1959. In addition, all properties in the state are destined to be revalued and reassessed this year at as yet undetermined percentages of their true value.

The state entered 1958 under the cloud of a national economic recession. By March the number of unemployed had climbed to 222,000, the highest since 1946. There were sharp cutbacks in defense spending and reduced workweeks were commonplace.

Meanwhile about five hundred of the state's major concerns, which had committed themselves to spend upward of $1 billion on new capital improvements by 1961, were seriously reviewing these pledges. Before midsummer several had either withdrawn their commitments or sharply reduced their capital programs.

Other needs of the state include more spending for the civil service and for welfare, better support for state colleges and the State University, improvement of parks, raising the level of mental care and of care for defective delinquents. For example, New York spends $1 per capita for the Community Mental Health Services Act. In New Jersey the total spent is the grand sum of 20 cents per capita.

Taking Pennsylvania, Delaware, Illinois, Indiana, Maryland, Michigan, New Jersey, New York, Ohio, and West Virginia as representative of the leading industrial states of the nation, we find New Jersey in the following categories:

Corporation "A"

The corporate characteristics as determined on the basis of five percentage relationships indicate three distinct types of corporate structures that must be considered. Corporation "A" is representative of industrial corporations which carry a relatively low level of inventories and a high level of investment in fixed assets. These industries have a relatively high income on sales and net worth and, as a consequence of the high investment in fixed assets, net income in relation to this item is low.

Corporation "B"

Corporation "B" is characteristic of industries which reflect approximately equal investments in fixed assets and in inventory. Their net income is low in relation to net sales and net worth, but higher than Corporation "A" in relation to investment in plant property and equipment. Property taxes for Corporation "B" would, therefore, be lower per dollar of net income than those of Corporation "A."

Corporation "C"

Corporation "C" is representative of industries which carry inventories relatively higher than their investment in fixed assets. While their net income return on sales and net worth is similar to that of Corporation "A," the income return in relation to the amount invested in plant property and equipment is high. Property taxes in relation to net income would thus be lower than for either "A" or "B."

State and Local Taxation as Basis

The percentage relationships used in establishing the three hypothetical corporations correspond with the factors of corporate structure which are the usual bases of state taxation. These are the corporate net worth or par or appraised value of the capital stock; the gross sales or gross receipts; and the corporate net income. There are variations among states in determining the tax bases, in the tax rates, and in the application of the tax rates to the tax base.

TABLE X

TOTAL AVERAGE STATE AND LOCAL TAXES
PER $1,000 OF NET PROFIT

Rank	State	Corporation "A" (Net Profit $2,025,000)
1.	Michigan	$116.34
2.	Maryland	$110.96
3.	Indiana	$ 93.55
4.	New York	$ 91.02
5.	Pennsylvania	$ 84.22
6.	New Jersey	$ 64.26
7.	West Virginia	$ 57.39
8.	Illinois	$ 54.32
9.	Ohio	$ 52.76
10.	Delaware	$ 22.76

Rank	State	Corporation "B" (Net Profit $1,614,000)
1.	Michigan	$149.38
2.	Maryland	129.82
3.	Indiana	124.36
4.	West Virginia	77.21
5.	Pennsylvania	74.09
6.	New York	71.33
7.	New Jersey	68.93
8.	Illinois	65.62
9.	Ohio	64.91
10.	Delaware	12.53

Rank	State	Corporation "C" (Net Profit $1,900,500)
1.	Michigan	$123.36
2.	Maryland	119.64
3.	Indiana	103.79
4.	Pennsylvania	76.67
5.	New York	73.25
6.	West Virginia	62.52
7.	New Jersey	58.63
8.	Ohio	55.74
9.	Illinois	54.08
10.	Delaware	12.49

This table was computed before the new corporation tax was added to the list of state taxes. I still believe that a $1\frac{3}{4}$ per cent rate on corporate net income would not raise our position significantly.

This is due mainly to the low level of governmental services provided by New Jersey and is representative of the sharp differences in the cost of government in various localities. Newark has some of the highest tax rates in the nation. In other localities the rates may well be considerably less than those of Newark. This again suggests the need to find a basis for the taxation of all industrial property in the state on an even basis, so that when the state needs money it can tap all the industry evenly. The rise of bedroom communities has been a severe blow to the preservation of either high educational standards or high levels of general service. Many of these communities can-afford parks; cannot afford an adequate school system; many cannot afford decent roads.

If the State of New Jersey is to prosper, we need to have some broad-based tax that will keep pace with inflation, if inflation is to be the rule. We need to find means of improving educational standards in the poorer sections of the state. We need to find the revenue to purchase parks. We need to find the funds to improve the quality of state colleges and the State University. We need to find money to finance a more adequate program of mental health and the improvement in our state hospitals. We must spend more for water. We need a better highway system. Above all, we need planning, so that some of the needs of the state government can be anticipated and land can be purchased before the price becomes prohibitive.

As New Jersey is one of the wealthier states of the nation, there is no reason why we cannot afford a high quality of state services. Before this can be achieved the tax receipts must be increased sufficiently to finance a more adequate program. But at present the prospect of getting a better tax system seems remote. If we are to continue to prosper we must advance the quality of both state and local government—even if it costs money.

A general survey of the tax structure of the state and a complete revision must be based on the best evidence obtainable. No one in the state government is in a position to do this work. We should hire an outside expert to report on the state tax system and then follow his advice. There are many individuals who could do this job.

If we do not soon raise the level of state services, New Jersey will find that it has lost not only industry but also the talent to be found in its schools and colleges, and in research. However, the basic need is complete reform of the revenue system of the state. But so long as the press and the leaders in business and industry continue to sell the program of "no new taxes," there is great danger of a decline in the quality of state services, at the cost of attracting to the state the industries we want and need.

Much of what has been said shows the need to give up the property tax as the prime supporter of state services and to find a basis for another source of revenue. The variety of such measures available should make this a fairly simple job. But if such an attempt is to be made the resistance of the property taxpayer must be broken down so that his full support will be behind the movement. Certainly the property taxpayer now feels that he has been abused. The number of school budgets that failed in 1958 and 1959 is an indication of this fact. But so long as he has to pay the exhorbitant rates on his home there will be little chance of enlisting his support for reform of the state's tax system.

The tax on personality both in the plants of the state and on the household should be repealed. This tax is a joke in most of the jurisdictions that levy it. The tax on business property raises a lot of money, but if we found another source it too could be repealed. There should also be a marked reduction in the level of taxation of the railroads, to improve their chance of survival.

New Jersey must make its decision soon. Both the quality of our state government's services to the people and the quality of its industrial potential depend on it. The problem is how to alert the people of the state so that from among them some leadership will arise. The only well-organized group seemingly conscious of this crisis, and alerting its own members, is the League of Women Voters.

People who can lead the way should be appointed by the Governor, or there should be a commission set up by the Legislature. Otherwise they will not have the status and backing to be effective.

One difference between the League's program and mine is that the League believes it can achieve a personal income tax sooner than I think it will be possible. There is no doubt that it is a superior tax. But there is the federal burden to be considered, and the resistance to any more taxation of this sort. But sooner or later, tax reform has to come if our state is to keep and improve its position among the states of the Union.